Façon de Parler 1

Angela Aries & Dominique Debney

Study Guide

Hodder & Stoughton

A MEMBER OF THE HODDER HEADLINE GROUP

Contents

Orders: please contact Bookpoint Ltd,130 Milton Park, Abingdon, Oxon OX14 4SB. Telephone
(44) 01235 827720. Fax: (44) 01235 400454. Lines are open from 9.00-6.00, Monday to
Saturday, with a 24 hour message answering service. You can also order through our
website at www.madaboutbooks.com

British Library Cataloguing in Publication Data
A catalogue record for this title is available from The British Library.

First published 1986, second edition 1997
Third edition published 2000

Impression number   10 9 8 7
Year   2005 2004 2003

Copyright © 2000 Angela Aires and Dominique Debney

Typeset by Transet Limited, Coventry, England
Printed in Great Britain for Hodder & Stoughton Educational,
338 Euston Road, London NW1 3BH by The Bath Press, Bath.

Key

Première unité

à vous! (p.4)   **1** Bonjour, mademoiselle. **2** Bonjour, monsieur. **3** Bonjour, madame. **4** Bonjour, messieurs. **5** Bonjour, messieurs-dames.

avez-vous compris? (p.6)   Yves / Quimper; Henri; Luçon; Provence; Lucien; Annick / Bretagne; François; Marie / Alsace; Rouen; Antoine; Dominique / Corse.

à vous! (p.6)   **1** Je suis de Luçon. **2** Nous sommes de Quimper. **3** Je suis de Rouen. **4** Je suis de Paris. **5** Nous sommes de Strasbourg. **6** Je suis de Nuits-Saint-Georges. **7** Je suis de Grasse. **8** Nous sommes d'Ajaccio.

à vous! (p.9)   **1** Jeanne, **2** Yves et Annick, **3** Lucien et Josée, **4** Dominique et Antoine, **5** Henri, **6** Marie et François.

avez-vous compris? (p.10)   **1** faux (français), **2** vrai, **3** vrai, **4** faux (française), **5** faux (anglais), **6** vrai, **7** faux (américains), **8** faux (gallois).

☞ à vous! (p.11) **1** Elle est écossaise. **2** Elle est anglaise.
3 Il est suisse. **4** Il est allemand. **5** Elle est française. **6** Il est américain.
7 Il est français. **8** Ils sont russes. **9** Elles sont anglaises. **10** Elles sont
italiennes. **11** Ils sont français. **12** Ils sont indiens.

EXERCICES **A** e d a b c. **B 1** suis, **2** êtes, **3** suis,
4 êtes, **5** est, **6** suis. **C 1** Oui, elle est française. **2** Oui, il est français.
3 Non, il est allemand. **4** Oui, il est français. **5** Non, il est suisse. **6** Non,
il est américain. **7** Non, ils sont anglais. **8** Oui, elle est française. **9** Oui,
elles sont françaises. **10** Oui, il est français. **11** Non, il est africain.
12 Non, il est australien. **D 1** Comment vous appelez-vous? **2** Vous êtes
français? / Est-ce que vous êtes français? **3** D'où êtes-vous? / Vous êtes d'où?
E 1 italien, **2** gallois, **3** suisse, **4** belge, **5** espagnol, **6** anglais,
7 allemand, **8** irlandais. *Fem:* **1** italienne, **2** galloise, **3** suisse, **4** belge,
5 espagnole, **6** anglaise, **7** allemande, **8** irlandaise.

🎧 écoutez bien! **Deuxième partie 1** c, **2** c, **3** a, **4** b, **5** a,
6 b, **7** c, **8** a.

Deuxième unité

 avez-vous compris? (p.16) **1** c, **2** d, **3** e, **4** a, **5** f, **6** b.

 à vous! (p.16) **1** mariée, **2** marié, **3** célibataire,
4 célibataires, **5** petit ami **6** fiancés, **7** divorcé.

avez-vous compris? (p.19)   Only Annick and François' statements are not correct.

EXERCICES   **B 1** Daniel, **2** Nicole, **3** Charlotte, **4** Bruno, **5** Anne, **6** Guy. **C 1** est, **2** est, **3** est, **4** sont, **5** est, **6** sont, **7** est, **8** est, **9** sommes. **D 1** Je m'appelle Brown. Non, je ne suis pas canadien, je suis américain. Non, je ne suis pas célibataire, je suis marié. Non, elle n'est pas américaine, elle est chinoise. Je travaille en plein air. **2** Je m'appelle Tania. Non, je ne suis pas française, je suis russe. Oui, je suis de Moscou. Oui, je suis mariée. Je travaille dans un hôpital. **3** Oui, nous sommes allemands. Oui, nous sommes de Berlin. Oui, nous sommes mariés. Nous sommes professeurs. **4** Non, nous ne sommes pas écossais, nous sommes gallois. Non, nous ne sommes pas de Cardiff, nous sommes de Cardigan. Nous sommes fonctionnaires.

écoutez bien! **1** Henri and Jeanne. Their names. **2** Where they come from. One is from Bastia in Corsica, and the other one from London. **3** Who the third person is, and if he's the guide. The person says he doesn't know. **4** Both are single but the second one has a German boyfriend. **5** Their jobs. One is a fisherman, the other a factory worker. **6** She works in a hospital. She is a doctor.

Troisième unité

 avez-vous compris? (p.29)   Five people have chosen alcoholic drinks.

 avez-vous compris? (p.30)   cheese, ham, paté and toasted ham and cheese.

 à vous! (p.30)   Claire / François / Josée / Guillaume / Lucien / Marie.

 avez-vous compris? (p.32)   **Children** Claire: 1 son, Paul; 1 daughter, Élisabeth. Henri: none. Marie et François: 2 children. **Pets** Claire: white mice, 1 rabbit, 1 hamster, goldfish. Henri: 1 cat called Moustache. Marie et François: 1 guinea pig
Accommodation Claire: flat in Rouen. Henri: small house in Nuits-Saint-Georges. Marie et François: flat in Strasbourg.

 à vous! (p.33)   **1** – Vous avez un animal familier? / – J'ai des poissons rouges. **2** – Avez-vous des enfants? / J'ai une fille. **3** – Vous avez un appartement / – J'ai une maison. **4** – Vous avez un chien? / – Non mais j'ai deux chats.

 avez-vous compris? (p.34)   **1** voiture, **2** moto (*false*), **3** bateau / camion, **4** vélo, **5** garage (*false*), **6** mobylette.

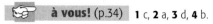 **à vous!** (p.34)   1 c, 2 a, 3 d, 4 b.

avez-vous compris? (p.35)   50 bouteilles de vin, 10 bouteilles de Chablis, 1 bouteille de Meursault, 4 bouteilles de Volnay.

EXERCICES   **A 1** Bonsoir monsieur. **2** Un verre de vin blanc pour moi, s'il vous plaît. **3** Une bière pour monsieur / madame / mademoiselle. **4** Bouteille. **5** Trois schweppes, cinq cocas et sept citrons pressés. **6** Oui, nous sommes professeurs. **B 1** c, **2** e, **3** d, **4** a, **5** b. **D 1** ai / a, **2** ont, **3** Avez/avons, **4** a / ai, **5** avez / avons / avons, **6** as / ai. **E 1** sept, neuf, **2** vingt, **3** quatorze, seize, dix-huit, **4** dix-sept, seize, quinze, **5** treize, onze.

écoutez bien! **Première partie 1** 11€, **2** 14€, **3** 50€, **4** 19€, **5** 12,50€. **Deuxième partie a** faux, **b** vrai, **c** faux, **d** vrai, **e** faux, **f** vrai.

Faites le point! (unités 1–3)

1 a sont / sont, **b** sommes / sommes, **c** êtes / suis / suis, **d** C'est / n'est pas / secrétaire, **e** Qui est-ce? / Il est / n'est pas / est. **2 a** ouvrière, **b** alsaciens, **c** Quel est votre métier? **d** Je m'appelle Jeanne. **e** célibataire. **3 a** un kir, **b** un café, **c** un vin rouge, **d** une bière pression, **e** No, **f** un sandwich au fromage. **4 a** un kir (the others are vehicles), **b** un fils (the others are animals), **c** une bouteille (the others are related to buildings), **d** des amis (the others are animals), **e** un camion (the others are drinks), **f** une fille (the others are male relatives). **5 a** avons, **b** ont, **c** a, **d** ai, **e** ai. **a** (iii), **b** (v), **c** (i), **d** (ii), **e** (iv).

Quatrième unité

avez-vous compris? (p.44)   **1** la Seine, **2** les Invalides, **3** le quartier Latin, **4** l'île de la Cité, **5** le Centre Pompidou, **6** le palais de Chaillot, **7** la Défense.

à vous! (p.44)   **1** c'est une cathédrale. **2** c'est un musée. **3** C'est une église. **4** (ce n'est pas une église), c'est un hôpital. **5** C'est un théâtre. **6** C'est un bateau.

avez-vous compris? (p.46)   **1** the north of Paris, **2** artists, **3** le Printemps and les Galeries Lafayette, **4** a theatre, **5** a palace, **6** an Egyptian obelisk, from Luxor, **7** a traffic jam.

à vous! (p.46)   **1** c, **2** b and d, **3** f and g, **4** a, **5** e, **6** h.

avez-vous compris? (p.49)   **1** one night, **2** shower, washbasin, toilet, television and telephone, **3** 182 euros, **4** in the car park, **5** 610, on the sixth floor, **6** the lift is out of order.

à vous! (p.49)   **1 a** Une chambre pour deux personnes, avec douche, pour deux nuits. **b** Une chambre pour une personne, avec lavabo et WC privés, pour une nuit. **c** Une chambre pour deux personnes, avec salle de bain et télévision, pour trois nuits. **d** Une chambre pour une personne, avec douche et téléphone, pour une nuit.

EXERCICES

A 1 les portes, **2** l'escalier, **3** le couloir, **4** le balcon, **5** les fenêtres, **6** l'ascenseur, **7** les armoires, **8** la douche, **9** la salle de bain, **10** les tables. **B 1** un / un / des, **2** des, **3** un, **4** des, **5** une, **6** un. **C 1** chambres, **2** ce soir, **3** douche, **4** combien, **5** personne, **6** étage, **7** Il y a, **8** cent, **9** compris, **10** euros, **11** clé. **D 1** Qu'est-ce que c'est? (La Madeleine) **2** Qu'est-ce que c'est? (la place Vendôme) **3** Qui est-ce? (Molière) **4** Qu'est ce que c'est (La pyramide de verre) **5** Qui est-ce? (Renoir) **6** Qui est-ce? (Marie Curie) **7** Qu'est-ce que c'est? (l'Opéra)

écoutez bien!

Première partie une chambre, combien, ma femme, nuits, quatorze, salle de bain, douche, 100, 100, petit déjeuner, 15, il y a, je regrette, ça va, votre nom.

Deuxième partie 1 Y – I – O – A – U – H – R – W – J – X – K – V – E – T – G. **2** Lyon, Ajaccio, Tours, Strasbourg, Bordeaux, Quimper. Tours (s missing), and Bordeaux (e missing).

lecture

PRICES IN EUROS			
Tax and service <u>included</u>			
	1	2	Extra <u>bed</u>
	person	persons	
Room <u>with shower</u>	90,20	90,20	
Room <u>with bathroom</u>	100/140	100/140	50
<u>Suite</u>	250	250	
<u>Breakfast</u>	12,50	25	

HALF BOARD (minimum 3 days)		
Room <u>with bathroom</u>	145/170	175/190
<u>Suite</u>		220

FULL BOARD		
Room <u>with bathroom</u>	150/180	180/200
<u>Suite</u>		250

MENUS
<u>Children</u> 20€
35€ <u>except Sat. eve and Sundays</u>
40€, 48€, 55€ and à la carte

HOTEL SPORTS
Tennis <u>on artificial grass</u> Golf course with three greens, Jogging in the forest – <u>Mountain bikes</u>

Cinquième unité

 avez-vous compris? (p.58)   **1** Jeanne and Sylvie,
2 Dominique and Antoine, **3** soup, **4** because there aren't any salads,
5 Antoine and Dominique, **6** egg mayonnaise.

à vous! (p.58)   **1** de la salade de tomates, **2** de la soupe,
3 *exemple* du saucisson à l'ail, **4** *exemple* un œuf dur à la mayonnaise.

avez-vous compris? (p.60)   (vrai = *true*, faux = *false*)
1 vrai, **2** faux, **3** vrai, **4** faux, **5** faux.

à vous! (p.61)   Je voudrais du poulet / du poisson / des
frites / de la ratatouille / des légumes / du riz. Il n'y a plus de poulet /
plus de poisson / plus de frites / plus de ratatouille / plus de légumes /
plus de riz.

avez-vous compris? (p.62)   gruyère ✓, yogurts ✓,
oranges ✓, Burgundy wine ✓.

à vous! (p.63)   **1** Qu'est-ce que vous avez comme
fromages? **2** Qu'est-ce que vous avez comme gâteaux? **3** Qu'est-ce que
vous avez comme vin? **4** Qu'est-ce que vous avez comme viande?
5 Qu'est-ce que vous avez comme fruits?

EXERCICES   **A 1 d** ail, **e** des fruits, **f** des œufs.
2 c pain, **d** café, **e** des légumes, **f** des champignons. **3 c** confiture,
d camembert / fromage, **e** du poisson, **f** de la soupe. **4 a** lait, **b** des
croissants, **c** du vin, **d** de l'eau, **e** des saucisses. **B** (*Suggested answers:*)
1 Je voudrais de la moutarde et de l'huile. **2** Je voudrais du café et des
croissants. **3** Je voudrais de la soupe et du poisson. **C** Dans le frigidaire il
n'y a pas de beurre, (il n'y a) pas de fromage, (il n'y a) pas d'œufs, (il
n'y a) pas de viande, (il n'y a) pas de bière, (il n'y a) pas de lait.
D 1 de l', **2** d', **3** du, **4** de, **5** de, **6** du, **7** du, **8** de la, **9** de, **10** des,
11 des, **12** de la, **13** de la, **14** du, **15** de, **16** du, **17** du, **18** du, **19** de,
20 du, **21** d'. **E** The shopkeeper cannot provide: olive oil, bread, beer,
green salad, tea, milk. The customer could get: wine, fruit, vegetables,
mustard, coffee, cheese.

 écoutez bien!   **1** chicken, chips. **2** toast. **3** fruit salad.
4 hot chocolate, milk. **5** mushroom. **6** pears. **7** butter, strawberry jam.
8 grapefruit. **9** soup. **10** beer. **11** mustard. **12** bread. **13** ham, cheese.
14 lemon tea. **15** fish, chips.

lecture   **1** à l'Epi d'or, **2** l'Océane, **3** à l'Epi d'or,
4 à la Grande Chute, **5** la Tanière, **6** à la Grande Chute, **7** Les Marmottes
and à la Grande Chute, **8** Les Marmottes, **9** à la Grande Chute,
10 Le Yéti.

Sixième unité

à vous! (p.72) **a** a, **b** a, ans, **c** ont, **d** avez, **e** avons, **f** mois, **g** as, **h** ai, **i** âge, **j** quel, a.

à vous! (p.73) **1** faim, **2** soif, **3** chance, **4** sommeil, **5** peur, **6** chaud.

avez-vous compris? (p.75) **1** Non. **2** Non. **3** Non. **4** Une araignée. **5** Non. **6** Non. **7** Entre le sac et la valise. **8** Oui.

à vous! (p.76) **1** dans, **2** sous, **3** au mur, **4** un vélo, **5** sur, **6** par terre, **7** au plafond, **8** devant, **9** entre, **10** dans.

avez-vous compris? (p.78) **1** faux, **2** faux, **3** vrai, **4** vrai, **5** faux, **6** faux.

à vous! (p.78) **a** (vi), **b** (iv), **c** (i), **d** (iii), **e** (v), **f** (ii), **g** (viii), **h** (vii), **i** (x), **j** (ix). **2** le vélo de l'infirmière, l'avion du pilote, la moto de l'ingénieur, le tracteur du fermier, le camion de l'ouvrier, le car du guide, la voiture de la famille, la caravane des touristes, la tente des étudiants.

EXERCICES **A 1** g, **2** d, **3** a, **4** h, **5** c, **6** e, **7** b, **8** f. **B 1** un chien. **2** dans le ciel. **3** une voiture. **4** entre les arbres. **5** devant l'école. **C** (*Suggested answers*) Le sac est par terre. Les clés sont dans le tiroir. Le parapluie est contre le mur. Les lunettes sont dans la boîte. Les crayons sont sur la table. Le chat est sous la chaise. **D 1** de, **2** du, **3** de la, **4** de la, **5** du, **6** de, **7** des, **8** du, **9** de l'. **E 1** 90; **2** 80, 100; **3** 96; **4** 61, 71, 81, 91; **5** 75, 70, 65, 60.

écoutez bien! **Première partie 1** eight, 16; **2** 17, 14; **3** six months; **4** sisters; **5** thirsty; **6** hot. **Deuxième partie 1** Glasses, on the desk between the lamp and the magazine. **2** Pen, in the bedside table drawer. **3** Umbrella, on the floor in front of the radiator. **4** Car keys, in the bag. **5** Fifi the dog, under the bed in the bedroom.

Faites le point! (unités 4–6)

1 a parapluie, **b** douches, **c** pêcheur, **d** carte, **e** champignon, **f** pont, **g** fleur, **h** embouteillage. **2 a** désirez, **b** il y a, **c** dix-sept, **d** seize, **e** chance, **f** étage, **g** ascenseur, **h** faim, **i** soif, **j** clés. **3 a** des livres, des journaux, des magazines; **b** des croissants, du pain, des gâteaux; **c** du thé, du vin, du café; **d** des tomates, de la viande, des frites. **4** du poisson ✓, des fruits ✓, du fromage ✓, des œufs ✓, de la viande ✓. **5 a** sur, **b** derrière, **c** devant, **d** entre. **6 a** du professeur, **b** du pêcheur, **c** de la secrétaire, **d** de l'infirmière, **e** du médecin. **7 a** araignée, **b** tableau, **c** parapluie, **d** tiroir, **e** table.

Septième unité

 avez-vous compris? (p.88)   **1** because he is hungry, **2** a cake shop, **3** 100 metres away, **4** so that he can buy cigarettes, **5** next to the café, **6** no, five minutes away.

à vous! (p.89)   **1** dentifrice, pharmacie; **2** argent, banque; **3** timbres, poste; **4** chambre, hôtel; **5** légumes, marché; **6** soif, café; **7** pain, boulangerie; **8** librairie, livre; **9** faim, gâteau.

avez-vous compris? (p.92)   **1** the Rex Cinema, **2** far, **3** five minutes, **4** traffic lights, **5** cross over, **6** on the left, **7** on the right, **8** straight on.

à vous! (p.92)   **a** prenez, **b** gauche, **c** première, **d** droite, **e** Traversez, **f** place, **g** tout, **h** jusqu'à, **i** Tournez, **j** croisement.

avez-vous compris? (p.96)   **1** Il est entre la place de la Concorde et le Louvre. **2** Il y a l'obélisque de Louqsor. **3** Non, elle est à côté des Tuileries. **4** Le palais de l'Unesco est près de l'École Militaire. **5** Il y a la Madeleine, la place Vendôme, le boulevard Haussmann et les grands magasins. **6** Ils sont dans la première rue à droite de l'hôtel.

EXERCICES   **A 1** piscine, Tournez à droite.
2 supermarché, Allez / Continuez tout droit, tournez à gauche. **3** poste, prenez la deuxième (rue) à gauche, la première (rue) à droite. **4** gare, Traversez la place, allez / continuez tout droit, tournez à droite.

B 1 Pardon madame, je cherche le centre commercial. **2** Pour aller à l'hôpital, s'il vous plaît? **3** C'est loin? **4** Je suis à pied. Il y a un bus? **5** Où est l'arrêt? **6** Où est le cinéma? **7** Merci. Au revoir madame. **C 1** L'église, **2** La piscine, **3** Le stade, **4** Le collège, **5** une station-service. **D 1** A côté de l'école. **2** Il y a une pharmacie en face de la boulangerie. **3** Oui, elle est près du parking. **4** Non, il est loin d'ici, au nord de la ville, à dix kilomètres. **5** Au milieu de la place. **6** Allez jusqu'aux feux, tournez à gauche, puis prenez la deuxième à droite. **7** À cinq minutes à pied. **8** Vous y êtes!

écoutez bien! Première partie 1 e, **2** a, **3** d, **4** b, **5** c, **6** f.
Deuxième partie 1 ✓ **2** ✓ **3** ✗ **4** ✓ **5** ✓ **6** ✓ **1** Post Office, **2** swimming pool, **3** police station, **4** supermarket, **5** chemist's, **6** castle.

lecture **1** Hôtel les Fleurs (*The Flowers*), **2** La Combe Humbert (*Humbert's Coomb*) or Alpen Roc (*Alpen Rock*), **3** Fleur des Neiges (*Snow Flower*), **4** Les Dents Blanches (*The White Teeth*), **5** Dixie Bar, **6 a** Le Clin d'Œil (*The Wink*), **b** La Rotonde (*The Rotunda*).

Huitième unité

 avez-vous compris? (p.102) **1** vrai, **2** faux, **3** vrai, **4** vrai, **5** faux.

 avez-vous compris? (p.104) **1** vrai, **2** faux, **3** vrai, **4** faux, **5** faux.

 avez-vous compris? (p.106) **1** faux, **2** faux, **3** vrai, **4** faux, **5** vrai.

 à vous! (p.106) **1** e, **2** f, **3** d, **4** a, **5** b, **6** c.

 avez-vous compris? (p.108) **1** la SNES, **2** Rouen, **3** Rouen, **4** du poisson, **5** les sardines, **6** Chantal.

 avez-vous compris? (p.109) **1** non, **2** oui, **3** non, **4** non.

 avez-vous compris? (p.112) **1** Oui, elle habite Rouen depuis vingt-cinq ans. **2** Elle a deux filles. **3** Elles ont dix-neuf et vingt ans. **4** Non, elles ne travaillent pas, elles étudient à l'université. **5** Elles habitent à Paris. **6** Oui, elles sont musiciennes. Sophie joue de la guitare et Nicole joue du piano. **7** Elles aiment la natation et elles jouent au tennis. **8** Elle aime chanter les airs de la Compagnie Créole.

à vous! (p.112) **1** Oui, ils étudient à l'université de Dijon.
2 Oui, ils habitent à Dijon. **3** Ils préfèrent Paris. **4** Ils aiment le sport, ils
jouent au tennis. **5** Martin joue de la guitare et Martine chante.

EXERCICES   **A** (*Suggested answers*) Où habitez-vous?
Où travaillez-vous? Aimez-vous le sport? Jouez-vous du piano? Est-ce
que vous regardez la télévision? Vous mangez souvent du poisson, de la
viande, du fromage? **B 1** Ils travaillent dans un bureau. **2** J'habite au
bord de la mer. **3** Elle aime la musique moderne. **4** Ils étudient l'anglais.
5 Nous jouons de la guitare. **6** Il parle à Chantal à la pause-café. **7** Je
regarde la télé seulement le soir. **8** Nous écoutons la radio. **9** Elle achète
le poisson au marché. **10** Je mange un sandwich le midi. **C** (*Suggested
answer*) Chère Marie-Pascale, Bonjour! Je m'appelle Sylvia. J'ai vingt-et-
un ans et j'habite dans une maison à Finchley, près de Londres. Je
travaille dans un grand magasin à Londres. Je suis mariée. Roger travaille
aussi à Londres, dans un bureau. Nous n'avons pas d'enfants, mais nous
avons un chien; il s'appelle Jacko. Et vous, êtes-vous mariée? Avez-vous
un chien? Aimez-vous le sport? Moi je joue au badminton et au ping-pong.

   J'aime la musique moderne et je joue de la clarinette et de la guitare.
Et vous, êtes-vous musicienne? Le soir j'écoute souvent la radio ou des
CD et je regarde quelquefois la télévision. Amicalement, Sylvia.
D (*Suggested answers*) **1** J'habite a Calcot. **2** C'est dans la banlieue de
Reading, dans le sud de l'Angleterre. **3** J'habite à Calcot depuis quinze
ans. **4** Oui. On peut jouer au tennis, au football, au badminton, faire de
la natation et de l'équitation. **5** Il y a deux écoles et trois églises. **6** On
peut visiter le château de Windsor et aller à Londres. **7** Il y a un centre
commercial, un parc et une rivière. **8** Oui, j'aime bien habiter à Calcot
parce que ce n'est pas loin de Londres et j'ai beaucoup d'amis.

écoutez bien! **1** habitez/habitons/banlieue, **2** travaillent/usine/ne/pas, **3** préfère/joue/chante, **4** parlez/allemand/étudie/espagnol, **5** aiment/adorent écouter/regarder, **6** achètes/mange/adore.

Neuvième unité

avez-vous compris? (p.117) **1** Elle fait un gâteau. **2** Les enfants font les devoirs. **3** Paul et Élisabeth font du bruit. **4** Ils font une erreur. **5** Il écoute les informations. **6** Oui, elle fait la cuisine. **7** Ils jouent au football. **8** L'été il fait du vélo, l'hiver il fait du ski. **9** Non, ils bavardent. **10** Elle tricote un pull-over.

à vous! (p.118) **1** faites, **2** faisons, **3** font, **4** font, **5** fais, **6** fais, **7** fais, **8** fais, **9** fait. **1** vrai, **2** faux, **3** faux, **4** faux, **5** vrai, **6** vrai, **7** vrai, **8** faux, **9** faux, **10** vrai.

à vous! (p.121) **1** cousines, **2** mère, **3** frère, **4** père, **5** sœur, **6** nièce, **7** tante, **8** grand-mère.

avez-vous compris? (p.122) (3, 5, 6, 7, 9, 10 are correct) **1** Colette a trois frères. **2** La sœur de Pierre a quatorze ans. **4** Louis et Françoise ont six petits-enfants. **8** Pierre et Annie ont un oncle. **11** Les petites-filles de Louis s'appellent Annie et Colette. **12** Cécile est la fille de Louis et Françoise.

avez-vous compris? (p.123)   **1.** Colette téléphone à une amie dans sa chambre. **2.** Grand-père chante dans la salle de bain. **3.** Philippe joue de la trompette. **4.** Grand-mère mange du chocolat en cachette dans sa chambre. **5.** Mme Dupré regarde la télé au salon. **6.** M. Dupré fait le ménage dans la salle à manger. **7.** Jean-Pierre épluche les pommes de terre dans la cuisine. **8.** Paul fait des devoirs dans la cuisine. **9.** L'oncle Jean goûte le cidre à la cave. **10.** Tante Cécile donne à manger aux volailles dans la basse-cour.

avez-vous compris? (p.125)   **1** Il a 3 chevaux, 20 vaches et 100 moutons. **2** Non, elle préfère les volailles. **3** Il y a des oies, des canards, un coq, des poules et des poussins. **4** Il regarde la moissonneuse-batteuse. **5** Ils préfèrent les machines.

à vous! (p.126)   12 poussins, 1 coq, 6 poules, 100 moutons, 1 chèvre, 4 canards, 10 cochons, 2 oies, 20 vaches, 3 chevaux.

EXERCICES   **A 2** Elle fait le ménage. **3** Elles bavardent. **4** Ils font la cuisine. **5** Il fait du ski. **6** Elle étudie. **7** Ils jouent au tennis. **8** Elle fait du vélo. **9** Elle tricote. **10** Elle mange. **11** Il fait des devoirs. **12** Il joue de la trompette. **B 1** mari, **2** frère, **3** cousine, **4** petite-fille, **5** beau-frère, **6** tante, **7** neveu, **8** femme, **9** belle-fille, **10** belles-sœurs. **C 1** J'habite dans la banlieue de Londres. **2** Un appartement. **3** Au deuxième étage. **4** Non, c'est petit. Qu'est-ce que c'est 'living-room' en français? **5** Merci. Il y a une salle de séjour, une chambre, une cuisine et une salle de bain. **6** Non, mais il y a un parking. **7** Non, mais il y a un arbre au milieu du parking! **D** La ferme est grande. Elle est à quarante kilomètres de Londres. Nous avons trente vaches, cinquante moutons et une centaine de cochons (environ cent cochons). Nous n'avons pas de chevaux. Venez avec moi, les enfants! Dans la basse-cour, il y a des poules et des poussins. Nous avons aussi des canards et des oies.

E (*Suggested answers*) **1** J'habite dans une maison. **2** Il y a la cuisine, la salle à manger et le salon. **3** Il y a trois chambres et la salle de bain. **4** Il y a un lit, deux tables de nuit, une armoire, une commode et un fauteuil. **5** Dans le salon. **6** Dans la cuisine. **7** J'aime lire, écouter de la musique ou regarder la télé. **8** Ma femme fait la cuisine. **9** Oui, nous avons un petit jardin. **10** Nous avons un garage et une cave. Dans le garage, il y a la voiture et les vélos. À la cave il y a du vin et des souris! **F** (*Suggested answer*) La maison de mes rêves est située au bord de la mer dans le sud de la France. Au rez-de-chaussée, il y a une cuisine moderne, un salon avec beaucoup de fauteuils confortables, une grande salle à manger et un bureau. Au premier étage, il y a cinq ou six chambres avec douche et deux salles de bain. Il y a un grenier, une cave avec beaucoup de bouteilles de vin et un garage avec deux ou trois voitures. Dans le jardin, il y a des arbres, des fleurs, une piscine et un court de tennis.

écoutez bien! **Première partie 1** Playing football in the garden. **2** Watching TV in the lounge. **3** On holiday in Brittany. **4** Working in the office. **5** Having a shower in the bathroom. **6** Cleaning the dining-room. **7** Making sandwiches in the kitchen.

Deuxième partie 1 brother, **2** mother, **3** parents-in-law, **4** father, **5** sister, **6** grand-mother, **7** children.

lecture (*Suggested answer*) **Gourin** – accommodates 7–8. Well-restored Breton dwelling, situated in a village.

Ground floor Living room, equipped kitchen, fireplace, lounge area, dining area, WC, bathroom, washing machine. *First floor* Two rooms with double beds, one room with three single beds. Loft fitted out as a games room. Enclosed garden, garden furniture. Shopping, swimming-pool, tennis – Gourin. Beach – le Pouldu. **Plouray** – accommodates 2–4. Breton dwelling tastefully restored, situated in the middle of the countryside at the end of a little track. *Ground floor* Large living room with fireplace, lounge furniture, sofa bed for two, dining area, equipped kitchen area, bathroom, separate WC. *First floor* One room with double bed, one with twin beds. Garden, one animal accepted. Shopping – Plouray, 5 km.

Faites le point! (unités 7–9)

1 a au milieu, **b** autour, **c** par terre. **2 a** quel, **b** où, **c** quelle, **d** à gauche. **3 a** Pardon monsieur, pour aller à la gare s'il vous plaît? **b** Oui, c'est loin? **c** Il y a un hôtel près de la gare? **d** Il y a un hôtel par ici? **e** Merci monsieur, au revoir. **4 a** par ici, **b** loin, **c** à pied, **d** tout droit, **e** Quelle, **f** à droite, **g** Traversez, **h** prenez, **i** à côté de. **5 a** le père, **b** la grand-mère, **c** la sœur, **d** le mari, **e** la tante. **6 a** Il fait du ski. **b** Elles font du bruit. **c** Ils font du vélo. **d** Ils font des devoirs. **e** Il fait la cuisine. **7 a** (ii), **b** (vi), **c** (v), **d** (i), **e** (iii), **f** (vii), **g** (iv), **h** (viii), **i** (x), **j** (ix). **8** The gîte at Hauteville-sur-mer will accommodate 6/7 people. It's a well-restored Normandy house situated right in the country at the end of a little lane. On the ground floor there's a living room with a sofa bed for one, a fitted kitchen, a lounge and dining area, toilet and bathroom. On the first floor there are two rooms with double beds, one with two singles. The garden is enclosed and one animal is allowed. The nearest shops are at Hauteville-sur-mer, which is 3 kilometres away or Coutances which is 15. There is a beach at Hauteville-sur-mer. **9** The farm is 20 kilometres from Arromanches. On the ground floor there is an enormous kitchen with a fireplace, lounge, living-room, dining-room and WC. On the first floor there are five bedrooms and a bathroom. The loft has been converted into a games room. There is a cellar and an enclosed garden. They have tractors and a combine-harvester. As far as animals are concerned, they have 20 cows, 4 horses and 25 pigs. They also have a cockerel, 30 hens, 15 geese and 18 ducks.

Dixième unité

avez-vous compris? (p.134) **1** Il fait froid. **2** Quelquefois il fait mauvais, il pleut. **3** En été, en général, il fait beau. **4** Il fait très chaud dans le désert. **5** Il fait souvent du vent en automne. **6** Il neige quelquefois en hiver. **7** En été, en général, il fait du soleil. **8** Il fait très chaud dans le désert. **9** Il fait froid en hiver. **10** Il pleut au printemps et en automne.

à vous! (p.135) **a** il pleut, **b** il fait froid, **c** il fait du brouillard, **d** il fait mauvais, **e** il neige, **f** il fait beau, **g** il fait du soleil, **h** il neige, **i** il fait chaud, **j** il fait du vent.

avez-vous compris? (p.136)   **1** Parce qu'il est à la retraite. **2** Il fait du jardinage. **3** Des fleurs et des légumes. **4** La pêche. **5** Aller aux escargots. Parce qu'il adore les escargots.

à vous! (p.137)   **1** J'ai soixante-dix ans. **2** Oui, je suis à la retraite depuis cinq ans. **3** Oui, j'ai de la chance! **4** Je fais du jardinage. **5** Il y a des fleurs et des légumes. **6** Aller à la pêche.

avez-vous compris? (p.138)   **1** Il va à la messe et au café. **2** Il joue de l'accordéon. **3** Au café, avec des amis. **4** Il prépare le dîner puis il regarde la télévision. **5** Les films d'aventure et les émissions pour les enfants. **6** Il a quatre-vingt-quinze ans.

à vous! (p.138)   **1** Je suis très occupé(e). **2** Je vais à la messe. **3** Je bois l'apéritif au café. **4** Je joue aux cartes avec des amis. **5** Non, mais je prépare le dîner tous les soirs. **6** Oui, sauf le samedi.

avez-vous compris? (p.140)   **1** Oui, il a une grande sœur et un petit frère. **2** Il joue au ballon, aux billes ou aux gendarmes et aux voleurs. **3** En général ils regardent la télévision, mais quelquefois ils jouent au ping-pong, au train électrique ou aux fléchettes. **4** Oui, il adore jouer avec l'ordinateur. **5** Elle est trop vieille. **6** Elle a quinze ans.

à vous! (p.140)   (*Suggested answers*) On joue au ballon, on joue aux fléchettes, on joue au ping-pong, on regarde la télé, on joue au train électrique, on joue aux billes.

avez-vous compris? (p.141)   **1** Oui, elle travaille à mi-temps. **2** Parce qu'elle a des enfants. **3** Elle aime lire le journal et faire les mots croisés. Elle aime aussi faire du crochet et de la couture. **4** Il fait collection de timbres. **5** Oui. Elle fait du yoga une fois par semaine. **6** Les garçons font du judo et les filles font de l'équitation. Et ils aiment tous la natation. **7** Non, il préfère regarder le sport à la télévision.

à vous! (p.142)   **1** pressée, **2** travail, **3** mi-temps, **4** lire, **5** mots croisés, **6** semaine, **7** promenade, **8** bois, **9** timbres, **10** sport, **11** natation, **12** fume.

EXERCICES   **A 1** En Normandie, **2** Dans les Alpes, **3** À la Martinique. **B 1** Je déteste repasser, faire la vaisselle et passer l'aspirateur. **2** Je n'aime pas faire une promenade quand il pleut. Je n'aime pas aller au lit tôt, lire le journal. **3** J'aime bien faire des mots croisés, faire du jardinage quand il fait beau, jouer aux cartes avec des amis. **4** Je préfère aller en vacances à l'étranger, voyager en voiture, regarder le sport à la télévision. **5** J'adore inviter des amis, bricoler, rester au lit tard le dimanche. **D 1** Où habitez-vous? **2** Est-ce que vous travaillez? **3** Qu'est-ce que vous faites quand vous avez du temps libre? **4** Qu'est-ce que vous aimez faire le soir quand vous ne regardez pas la télévision? **5** Est-ce que vous avez des enfants? **6** Comment s'appelle-t-elle? **7** Quel âge a-t-elle? **8** Fait-elle beaucoup de sport? **9** Et votre mari, il est sportif? **10** Quelles émissions préfère-t-il? **E** (*Suggested answer*) Chère Pascale, Merci de votre lettre. Nous aussi, nous sommes sportifs. Nous faisons de la natation toutes les semaines. L'été, nous jouons au tennis. L'hiver, Roger joue au football et moi je joue au badminton avec des amies. Le samedi soir nous allons quelquefois au restaurant. J'adore la cuisine chinoise mais Roger préfère la cuisine française traditionnelle. En général, nous restons à la maison le soir mais nous allons souvent au cinéma. Le mardi soir je fais mes devoirs d'anglais (le cours est le mercredi!) Le week-end, quand il fait beau, nous aimons rester dans le jardin. L'été il fait chaud, mais il pleut souvent au printemps est en automne. Nous avons de la chance parce qu'il ne fait pas trop froid l'hiver, mais le matin, il y a souvent du brouillard. Il neige rarement ici. Et vous, quel temps fait-il dans votre région? Écrivez-moi vite. Amicalement, Christine.

écoutez bien! You should have ticked: Aller à la piscine: de temps en temps; lire le journal: rarement; aller au cinéma: souvent; faire la cuisine: le samedi soir; faire la vaisselle: tous les soirs; aller à la montagne: quelquefois; aller à l'étranger: régulièrement; faire le jardinage: le dimanche; jouer aux cartes: une fois par semaine; aller à la pêche: jamais.

Onzième unité

avez-vous compris? (p.152)   **1** À sept heures. **2** À huit heures et quart. **3** François. **4** Elle fait la vaisselle. **5** À neuf heures. **6** Vers neuf heures et demie. **7** Au supermarché. **8** Quelquefois. **9** Elle range les achats. **10** Elle fait la lessive ou elle repasse. **11** Elle déjeune. **12** À deux heures.

 à vous! (p.152)   **1** d, **2** e, **3** c, **4** f, **5** a, **6** b.

avez-vous compris? (p.154) **1** Quatre. **2** Un rôti de bœuf. **3** Oui, pour six personnes. **4** Un pot de rillettes et un petit saucisson sec. **5** Parce qu'elle a des invités ce soir.

à vous! (p.154) **1** Bonjour, monsieur / madame. Vous désirez? **2** Comme ça? **3** Et avec ça? **4** Ça fait … Je voudrais un rôti de porc/un poulet/deux côtelettes d'agneau.

avez-vous compris? (p.156) **1** Quatre. **2** Environ une demi-livre. **3** Non, des yaourts nature. **4** Un litre de lait et un petit pot de crème fraîche. **5** Non, elle achète du beurre doux des Charentes.

à vous! (p.156) **1** Je voudrais un camembert, une tranche de roquefort et un beau morceau de gruyère. **2** Environ une demi-livre. **3** Je voudrais des yaourts. **4** Nature. **5** Neuf. Je voudrais aussi un pot de crème fraîche. **6** Oui. Ça fait combien?

avez-vous compris? (p.158) **1** kilos, **2** une salade de fruits, **3** un kilo, **4** 150 grammes, **5** n'achète pas.

à vous! (p.158) **1** voudrais, **2** combien, **3** voilà, **4** deux, **5** un, **6** grammes, **7** livre, **8** désirez, **9** tout.

à vous! (p.160) **1** beaucoup d', **2** trop de, **3** assez d'.

avez-vous compris? (p.162) **1** C'est le 17 mars. **2** Le 25 novembre. **3** Au mois d'août. **4** Le 12 juin. **5** Elle oublie toujours, elle ne sait pas.

👉 **à vous!** (p.162) **1** la Saint Valentin (*Valentine's Day*)
2 Mardi Gras (*Shrove Tuesday*) **3** Pâques (*Easter*) **4** la Fête du Travail
(*Labour Day*) **5** la Fête des Mères (*Mother's Day*) **6** la Fête des Pères
(*Father's Day*) **7** la Fête Nationale (*Bastille Day*) **8** la Toussaint (*All
Saints' Day*) **9** Noël (*Christmas*) **10** la Saint Sylvestre (*New Year's Eve*)
11 dimanche / mardi / mercredi **12** le samedi 20 mars / le lundi 21 juin /
le jeudi 23 septembre / le mardi 21 décembre.

EXERCICES   **A** Il est cinq heures, dix heures et quart,
huit heures vingt, cinq heures moins vingt, onze heures dix, huit heures
moins cinq, six heures cinq, deux heures moins le quart, une heure et
demie, trois heures moins dix, quatre heures vingt-cinq, midi (*or* minuit).
B 2 une tasse de thé, **3** un litre de lait, **4** un bol de café, **5** une cuillerée
d'huile, **6** un pot de confiture, **7** une livre de raisin, **8** des boîtes de
bière, **9** une bouteille d'eau, **10** un tonneau de cidre, **11** un paquet de
bonbons, **12** une assiette de soupe. **C 1** 1 **pot** de moutarde (1 cuillerée
à café), **2** 1 **douzaine** d'œufs (12 œufs), **3** 150 **litres** de lait (150 ml),
4 200 **kilos** de farine (200 grammes). **D 1** C'est mon tour. / C'est à moi.
Je voudrais une boîte de sardines à l'huile. **2** Je voudrais une bouteille
d'eau et un litre de vin rouge. **3** Oui, je voudrais aussi une demi-livre de
café et un kilo de sucre. **4** Est-ce que vous avez du pain? **5** Vous avez du
fromage? **6** Une tranche de roquefort, un petit fromage de chèvre et un
morceau de gruyère, s'il vous plaît. **7** C'est tout merci, ça fait combien?
E 1 C'est le vingt-neuf février. **2** Je m'appelle Dominique; c'est le huit
août. **3** Non, je suis célibataire. **4** Début juillet. **5** Du premier au quinze.
6 Quelquefois, je pars à Noël ou à Pâques. **7** Parce que j'adore le ski /
faire du ski.

écoutez bien! Première partie 1 9 heures, **2** vers 6 heures, **3** midi, **4** 1 heure, **5** 19 heures 30, **6** Quelquefois, **7** Supermarché, **8** dimanche matin, **9** mari, **10** 8 heures, **11** minuit, **12** minuit et demi, **13** Noël, **14** Pâques, **15** 6 heures du soir.

Deuxième partie 1 22€, **2** 19€, **3** 38€, **4** 61€, **15** 26€, **6** 4€50, **7** 25€, **8** 30€.

Douzième unité

 avez-vous compris? (p.172) **1** Elle attend le taxi. **2** Elle entend la voiture. **3** Elle prend l'appareil photo et le sac de voyage. **4** Elle descend vite l'escalier. **5** Pour aller à la gare.

 avez-vous compris? (p.173) **1** faux, **2** vrai, **3** vrai, **4** faux, **5** vrai.

 avez-vous compris? (p.175) **1** Ils prennent le train à huit heures. **2** Ils descendent du train. **3** Ils sont enfin au bord de la mer. **4** Ils laissent les bagages à l'hôtel. **5** Ils prennent l'appareil photo, les maillots de bain et une serviette.

 avez-vous compris? (p.176) **1** vrai, **2** vrai, **3** faux, **4** faux, **5** vrai.

 à vous! (p.177) **Belfry:** Easter till first Sunday of October.

10–12, 2–6. Closed Wednesday morning and Tuesday. **Museum of Fine arts:** 10–12, 2–6. Closed Wednesday morning and Tuesday. **Joan of Arc museum:** 9.30–6.30, from 1st April till 15th October. 10–12, 2–6.30 for the rest of the year. **Corneille museum:** 10–12, 2–6, closed on Thursdays, Friday morning, in November and certain public holidays.

avez-vous compris? (p.179)   **1** Ils font une promenade. **2** Il fait très beau. **3** Ils prennent beaucoup de photos. **4** Parce que la pellicule est finie. **5** Sur la plage. **6** Chantal prend un bain de soleil, et Laurent prend des photos de sa petite amie.

avez-vous compris? (p.181)   **1** Ils bavardent avec d'autres clients. **2** Ils visitent Dieppe. **3** Ils déjeunent dans un petit restaurant du port. **4** Ils écoutent les informations. **5** Non, les cheminots sont en grève.

à vous! (p.181)   **1** beau, **2** mer, **3** campagne, **4** appareil photo, **5** sac de voyage, **6** escalier, **7** gare, **8** bagages, **9** promenade, **10** pellicule.

EXERCICES   **A 1** apprend, **2** vend, **3** comprend, **4** prend, **5** descend, **6** répond, **7** attendre. **B 1** e, **2** g, **3** d, **4** h, **5** a, **6** c, **7** b, **8** f. **C 1** Le prochain train pour Dijon part à quelle heure? **2** Il arrive à Dijon à quelle heure? **3** De quel quai? **4** Trois billets s'il vous plaît. **5** Aller et retour. **6** Lundi soir. **D 1** attendez / attendons / attends, **2** vendez / vends / vendons, **3** entendez / entendons / entends, **4** répondez / répondons / réponds, **5** descendez / descends / descendons, **6** prenez / prends / prenons, **7** apprenez / apprenons / apprends, **8** comprenez / comprenons / comprends.

écoutez bien! **Première partie**

Destinations	Départs Paris	Arrivées
Annecy	7.24	10.59
Lausanne	12.25	16.06
Dijon	14.20	15.56
Macon	14.32	16.13
Genève	17.42	21.13
Berne	18.06	22.37

Deuxième partie 1 b (iii), **2** c (v), **3** d (iv), **4** a (ii), **5** e (i).

 lecture **1** Menthon, **2** Clermont, **3** Menthon, **4** either, **5** Menthon, **6** Clermont, **7** Menthon, **8** either.

Faites le point (unités 10–12)

1 a Il fait mauvais. Il pleut. **b** Il neige. **c** Il fait beau. Il fait du soleil. **d** Il fait du brouillard. **e** Il fait chaud. **f** Il fait du vent. **g** Il fait froid. **2 a** En général je suis en vacances en juin / au mois de juin. **b** Je prends souvent des photos. **c** Quelquefois je fais une promenade le dimanche. **d** Je joue rarement au tennis. **e** Je prends un bain tous les jours. **f** Je fais la cuisine de temps en temps. **g** Je ne prends jamais le bus. **h** Je fais les courses le matin. **i** Je ne regarde pas la télévision le samedi. **j** Je joue souvent de la guitare. **k** J'étudie le français une fois par semaine. **l** Je fais

toujours les devoirs. **3 a** neuf heures, **b** onze heures moins le quart,
c huit heures et quart, **d** deux heures et demie, **e** quatre heures moins dix.
4 a passe l'aspirateur, **b** fait la vaisselle, **c** fait la lessive, **d** repasse,
e prépare le déjeuner. **5 a** tasse, **b** boîtes, **c** bouteille, **d** verre, **e** tranche,
f pot, **g** paquet, **h** tonneau, **i** bol, **j** assiette. **6 a** le deux mai, **b** le vingt-trois
avril, **c** le quatorze juin. **d** le dix-sept juillet, **e** le premier janvier, **f** le quatre
février, **g** le dix-neuf septembre, **h** le vingt-et-un octobre, **i** le vingt-neuf
novembre, **j** le dix décembre. **7 a** vendez, vendons. **b** prenez, prends.
c attend, attend. **d** comprennent, comprennent. **e** vendez, vendent.
f descendez, descends, **g** apprenez, apprends. **h** réponds, réponds,
i prenez/prenons, **j** comprenez/comprends. **8 a** attend, **b** entend, **c** prend,
d descend, **e** attend, **f** décident, **g** comprennent. **9 De la** viande/**un**
jambon, **un** saucisson sec, **du** fromage, **une** baguette/**du** pain, **des** œufs,
des pommes, **du** raisin/**un** raisin, **des** pommes de terre, **un** pamplemousse,
un chou-fleur, **des** champignons, **des** fraises. **10 a** Bonjour monsieur.
b Je voudrais un kilo de pommes. **c** Une livre de raisin. **d** Deux
pamplemousses, un chou-fleur et deux cents grammes de champignons.
e C'est tout, ça fait combien? **f** Voilà monsieur, au revoir.

Treizième unité

avez-vous compris? (p.193)   Josée aime: le
chemisier, le pull-over, la veste, la robe, l'imperméable, le pantalon, la
robe du soir. Josée n'aime pas: la jupe, le tailleur, le corsage, le manteau.

à vous! (p.193)   **1** b, **2** e, **3** h, **4** j, **5** g, **6** c, **7** a, **8** d, **9** i, **10** f.

avez-vous compris? (p.194) **1** brown, navy blue, red. **2** beige, light grey. **3** dark grey, khaki. **4** orange, yellow. **5** pink. **6** black, brown.

à vous! (p.194) (*Suggested answers*) une robe bleu ciel, un chemisier blanc, un tailleur vert pomme, une jupe noire, un imperméable marron, un pull-over rose bonbon, une veste gris souris, un corsage rouge cerise, un pantalon jaune citron, une robe de soir lilas.

avez-vous compris? (p.195) **1** The suit and the raincoat. **2** The dress and the blouse. **3** Wool. **4** No, satin. **5** Synthetic fur. **6** The trousers. **7** With flowers. **8** Tartan.

à vous! (p.196) (*Suggested answers*) **1** Une robe en coton. **2** Une robe du soir en satin. **3** Une jupe en laine. **4** Un pantalon écossais. **5** Un pull-over en mohair. **6** Un chemisier à fleurs. **7** Un tailleur en velours. **8** Un manteau en tweed. **9** Un imperméable en polyester. **10** Une veste en soie.

à vous! (p.198) Lucien selected: the dinner jacket, the frilly shirt, the bow tie, the short jacket, the pink and white striped shirt, the maroon silk tie, the navy blue suit and a pair of jeans.

avez-vous compris? (p.198) **1** *jeans* = un blue-jean, **2** *short jacket* = un blouson, **3** *shirt* = une chemise ✓, **4** *dinner jacket* = un smoking, **5** *tie* = une cravate ✓, **6** *bow-tie* = un nœud papillon ✓ **7** *overcoat* = un pardessus, **8** *suit* = un costume ✓. à carreaux; à rayures; à pois; écossais; à fleurs; uni

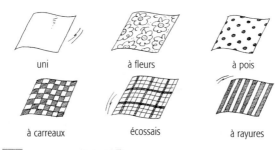

uni   à fleurs   à pois

à carreaux   écossais   à rayures

☞ **à vous!** (p.199)

Numéro de catalogue	Article	Taille	Couleur	Prix (Euros)
H 2 0 8	Robe	40	Abricot	150
P 1 7 0	Jupe	40	Écossaise	110
D 1 9 9	Pantalon	40	Marron	80
K 1 1 3	Imperméable	40	Gris foncé	190
V K 5 5	Chemise	G	Bleue	62
J K 8 1	Cravate		Bordeaux	55
			TOTAL	647

 avez-vous compris? (p.201) **1** verni, **2** ceinture,
3 chaussures, **4** véritable, **5** chapeau, **6** bottes.

 avez-vous compris? (p.203) Wool is too hot for
Martinique, doesn't like the colour, too smart, doesn't like checked
trousers, too expensive.

👉 **à vous!** (p.203) **1** Je cherche un imperméable. **2** Je déteste la couleur. **3** Vous avez quelque chose de moins cher? **4** Oui, il me plaît. **5** Je peux l'essayer? **6** Du quarante / quarante-deux, etc. **7** Merci monsieur / madame. Il coûte / fait combien?

💡 **avez-vous compris?** (p.205) **1** rouges, **2** 195€, **3** 38, **4** cuir véritable, **5** étroites, **6** cher.

👉 **à vous!** (p.205) **1** Vous désirez monsieur? **2** Les chaussures à cent cinquante euros? **3** Quelle est votre pointure? **4** Asseyez-vous. **5** Voilà, monsieur. **6** Oui, bien sûr.

EXERCICES   **A** (Any clothes that *you* would wear:) **1** for pottering about, **2** at work, **3** when it snows, **4** to eat out, **5** to work in the house or in the garden, **6** when it is hot, **7** at the seaside. **B 2** Le chapeau noir coûte cinquante-trois euros. **3** La jupe marron coûte soixante-seize euros. **4** Le manteau gris coûte deux cent quatre-vingts euros. **5** Le corsage à pois coûte quatre-vingt-deux euros. **6** La cravate rayée/à rayures coûte quarante-huit euros cinquante. **7** Le pantalon blanc coûte cent dix euros. **8** La robe à fleurs coûte cent trente-cinq euros. **C** Francine – valise 5; Brice – valise 1; Pascale – valise 2; Jean-Luc – valise 4; Marianne – valise 3. **D 1** Je cherche une veste. **2** En laine. **3** Je n'aime pas les vestes unies. **4** Je préfère la veste à carreaux. **5** Je fais du trente-huit / quarante, etc. **6** Non, c'est un peu trop cher pour moi.

🎧 **écoutez bien!** **1** vrai, **2** vrai, **3** faux, **4** faux, **5** faux, **6** faux, **7** faux, **8** vrai.

Quatorzième unité

avez-vous compris? (p.209) **1** a pen, **2** In his briefcase which is in the classroom. **3** They are sun-glasses; he is short-sighted. **4** He only needs to listen.

à vous! (p.210) **1 mon** stylo, bic; **ma** serviette; **mes** lunettes; **mes** lentilles de contact. **2 Mon** is used with masculine nouns, **ma** with feminine ones, and **mes** with nouns in the plural.

avez-vous compris? (p.211) **1** A beautiful leather one. **2** A translation. **3** No, she is hopeless. **4** She recognises the key ring. **5** He is slightly shortsighted. **6** She is shortsighted too. **7** They are in the language laboratory.

à vous! (p.211) **son** cahier, stylo; **sa** serviette, note; **ses** clés, lunettes. To translate *his/her* use **son** for masculine nouns, **sa** for feminine ones and **ses** for nouns in the plural.

avez-vous compris? (p.212) **1** sa serviette, **2** la salle de classe, **3** en cuir, **4** noire.

à vous! (p.213) d, a, e, c, b.

avez-vous compris? (p.215) **1** Brand new, very comfortable and automatic. **2** It has broken down. **3** Happy. The factory

is new and ultra-modern. **4** They have been on strike for a week.
5 Prosperous. They have several branches abroad. **6** No. **7** He often
travels abroad. **8** Only in Europe. **9** She speaks three languages –
French, English and German. **10** All his secretaries are very pretty.

👉 **à vous!** (p.215)   **1** notre, **2** notre, **3** nos, **4** votre, **5** vos,
6 vos.

💡 **avez-vous compris?** (p.217)   **1** In the mountains.
2 The children and the pets. **3** No. Paul goes to secondary school and
Elisabeth goes to primary school. **4** They are very noisy with their music
and their pets. **5** They are looking after some friends' pets.

👉 **à vous!** (p.217)   **1** leur(s), **2** leur, **3** leurs, **4** leurs, **5** leurs.

EXERCICES   **A** (*Suggested answers*) **1** comptable,
2 célibataire, **3** anglaise, **4** l'Angleterre, **5** jouer au tennis, faire collection
de timbres. **B 1** tes, **2** ta, **3** tes, **4** ton, **5** tes. **C 1** son, sa, sa, ses; **2** son,
sa, ses; **3** son, sa, ses; **4** son, sa, ses; **5** son, sa, son. **D 1** votre, **2** vos,
3 votre, **4** votre, **5** notre, **6** nos, **7** notre, **8** leur, **9** leurs, **10** leur, **11** leurs.
E 1 ton, **2** mon, **3** mon, **4** ta, **5** ma, **6** tes, **7** son, **8** ses, **9** ma, **10** ma,
11 ta. **F 1** Pardon monsieur, j'ai perdu mon portefeuille. **2** Hier, dans le
train. **3** Il est grand, en cuir. **4** Il est brun/marron. **5** Il y a de l'argent,
deux billets (de train), des cartes de crédit et des photos.

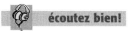

écoutez bien!

WHAT IS MISSING	PLACE LOST
umbrella	bus n° 16
suitcase	Don't know
bathing costume	**swimming-pool**
handbag	castle or museum
cat	market near fish stall

DESCRIPTION
yellow and green stripes
big, blue
pink and blue with flowers
red leather
called Mimi – 1 year old – black and white

Quinzième unité

 à vous! (p.222) **1** va, **2** vont, **3** va, **4** va, **5** va, **6** vont, **7** vont, **8** va, **9** vont.

 avez-vous compris? (p.223) **1** En train. **2** En bus. **3** Parce que les cheminots sont en grève. **4** 25 minutes. **5** Il ne sait pas.

avez-vous compris? (p.224) **1** À l'école. **2** À pied.
3 Seulement le mardi. **4** Parce que leur mère n'est pas à la maison.
5 Non, ils emportent toujours un sandwich.

 avez-vous compris? (p.225) **1** Faire les commissions
au supermarché. **2** Le mercredi. **3** En vélo. **4** La batterie de sa voiture est
à plat. **5** Il pleut.

 avez-vous compris? (p.226) **1** Elle est en vacances.
2 Les randonnées à cheval. **3** Rester en France. **4** Elle a peur. **5** Elle a le
mal de l'air. **6** Elle a le mal de mer. **7** C'est très rapide. **8** Il y a beaucoup
de grèves.

à vous! (p.226) J'ai horreur de voyager: **1** c, **2** a, **3** e, **4** d,
5 b. J'aime voyager: **1** c, **2** d, **3** a, **4** e, **5** b.

 avez-vous compris? (p.228) **1** Oui, très bien. **2** De
Paris. **3** Comme ci comme ça. **4** Elle est fatiguée. **5** Non, ils sont
malades, ils ont les oreillons. **6** Elle est vieille. **7** Non, elle est en panne.
8 Il est mort. **9** Il est au chômage. **10** Elle est en pleine forme.

à vous! (p.229) **1** Ça ne va pas! **2** Ça va! **3** Ça ne va pas!
4 Ça ne va pas! **5** Ça ne va pas! **6** Ça va! **7** Ça va! **8** Ça va!

EXERCICES **A** Je vais …, Tu vas …, Il va …,
Elle va …, Nous allons …, Vous allez …, Ils vont … **B 1** vas, **2** vais,
3 va, **4** va, **5** allez, **6** allons, **7** va, **8** va, **9** allons, **10** allez. **C 1** Ils y vont
deux fois par semaine. **2** J'y vais à pied. **3** Elle va très bien. **4** Nous

allons en Espagne. **5** Il va voir les vaches. **6** Elles vont voir le match de football. **7** Nous allons au lit. **8** Il y va du mardi au vendredi. **9** Elle va au supermarché. **10** Je vais boire une bière. **D** (*Suggested answer*) Cher Didier, Comment vas-tu? Moi, je suis un peu fatigué mais, heureusement, je vais partir en vacances la semaine prochaine. Je vais aller dans un petit hôtel dans le Midi et je vais y rester deux semaines. J'espère qu'il va faire beau et chaud. Je vais aller à la plage, je vais faire des promenades, je vais visiter les endroits intéressants et je vais prendre beaucoup de photos. Je vais manger au restaurant tous les jours – j'adore les spécialités de la région. Je vais aussi jouer au tennis et, avec un peu de chance, je vais rencontrer la femme idéale! Amitiés, Thomas P.S. Je vais t'envoyer une carte postale.

écoutez bien! The twins travel by coach, Gilles on the underground, Suzanne walks and takes a taxi, Bernard goes by plane, Alain by bicycle, Sabine by car.

lecture **1** Crédit Mutuel, **2** Morz'na Sports. **3** Au Plateau de Savoie, **4** Droguerie Morzinoise, **5** Droguerie Morzinoise or Librairie Passaquin, **6** Librairie Passaquin, **7** Garage Thiollay, **8** Momo Cheraiet, **9** Pizza Express, **10** Morz'na Sports.

Faites le point! (unités 13–15)

1 a votre ville, **b** vos bureaux, **c** votre usine, **d** votre café, **e** nos amis.
2 a leur fils, **b** leur fille, **c** leurs enfants, **d** ses parents, **e** ses parents.
3 a sa chemise est blanche, **b** sa cravate est rouge, **c** son pull-over est

jaune, **d** son pantalon est gris, **e** ses chaussures sont brunes / marron.
4 a chance, **b** malade, **c** belle-mère, **d** panne, **e** chômage. **5 a** blancs,
b longue, **c** noir, **d** en daim, **e** à fleurs, **f** en cuir. **6 a** Une robe en soie,
b une veste en fourrure synthétique, **c** une chemise rayée, **d** un
pantalon marron / brun, **e** une jupe longue, **f** des bottes blanches,
g une cravate à fleurs, **h** des chaussures vernies, **i** des gants de laine,
j une ceinture de cuir. **7 a** allons, en; **b** vont, en; **c** allez, à; **d** vais, en;
e vas, à. **8 a** Comment allez-vous? / Comment vas-tu? Comment ça va?
b Ils sont en grève. **c** Ma voiture est en panne. **d** Je suis pressé(e). **e** Il
est à l'étranger. **f** Il va à la piscine toutes les semaines. **9 a** (iv), **b** (vii),
c (i), **d** (iii), **e** (v), **f** (ii), **g** (viii), **h** (vi).

Seizième unité

avez-vous compris? (p.239) You should have ticked:
1 après, **2** le gérant, **3** Valette, **4** une nouvelle voiture / une voiture toute
neuve, **5** de sans plomb, **6** sale, **7** les pneus, **8** On peut.

à vous! (p.239) **1** (Faites) le plein, s'il vous plaît! **2** De
super / de sans plomb. **3** Ce n'est pas la peine. **4** Non, ça va! **5** Oui, il
est sale.

avez-vous compris? (p.241) **1** Depuis plusieurs mois.
2 Au cinéma ou chez des amis. Ils passent le week-end au bord de la
mer. **3** Laurent finit à 6 heures, et Chantal à 7 heures et demie. **4** Pour

aller à leur cours d'anglais. **5** Un quart d'heure avant le début du cours.
6 Il n'est pas fort en anglais, et il est un peu timide. **7** Il dort.

 à vous! (p.242) **1** c, **2** d, **3** f, **4** g, **5** a, **6** e, **7** b, **8** h.

 avez-vous compris? (p.243) You should have ticked:
1 vite, **2** n'a pas le temps, il sort, **3** ment, **4** de frites, de hamburgers,
5 n'intéressse pas.

avez-vous compris? (p.244) **1** Non, depuis deux ans
seulement. **2** Depuis le mois de septembre. **3** Oui, parce qu'il voit
beaucoup de monde. **4** Depuis six mois. **5** Non, seulement depuis
l'année dernière.

EXERCICES **A 1** Oui, ils grandissent vite. **2** Non, ils se
nourrissent de frites et de chocolat. **3** Ils sortent tous les soirs.
4 Damien, mon petit-fils, ne finit jamais ses devoirs! **5** Damien aussi. Et il
ment! **B 1** travail, **2** station-service, **3** plein, **4** gérant, **5** huile / eau,
6 eau / huile, **7** pneus, **8** pare-brise, **9** peine, **10** voiture.
C (*Suggested answer*) Londres, le 4 octobre …
Cher Pascal, Je t'écris cette lettre pour te présenter la famille Bickerton.
Ce sont des amis qui seront très contents de te recevoir pendant les
vacances de Noël. Tous les membres de la famille sont très
sympathiques. Ils habitent à Barnet, près de Londres, depuis douze ans.
Monsieur Bickerton est au chômage depuis deux ans. Madame Bickerton
travaille à mi-temps. Ils ne parlent pas français, mais ils adorent la
France. Leur fille, Susie, est mariée depuis trois mois et habite à Enfield

depuis son mariage. Leur fils, Timothy, a dix-sept ans. Il travaille dans une banque depuis un an, il a une moto et beaucoup d'amis. Pendant les week-ends, il joue au football; il est membre d'un club. Il adore aussi la pop musique. Il apprend à jouer de la guitare électrique depuis plusieurs mois. Je te souhaite de bonnes vacances en Angleterre. Amicalement,

écoutez bien! **1** A waiter in a small restaurant in Rouen. **2** About eight kilometres from the town centre. **3** By motorbike. **4** When the weather is really bad in winter, if it snows for instance. **5** Six o'clock. **6** Monday. **7** Saturday evening and Sunday lunch time. **8** Contact with people / nice colleagues. **9** Those who take ages to make up their mind, and those who don't say please and thank you. **10** About eleven at night. **11** They have a good cook at the restaurant, and he has his evening meals there. **12** She hates cooking.

lecture (*Suggested answer*) A large Renault stops outside a block of flats at one in the morning. The woman stays at the wheel while the man disappears into the building by the light of a torch. He breaks into one of the flats, goes into the bedroom and finds a lot of jewellery in the drawer of the bedside table. He empties it into a plastic bag and hurries off.

In a hotel in South America the same couple open a suitcase containing the plastic bag. As the man tips the jewellery onto the bed the woman realises all the pieces are fakes. On the bedside table there is a newspaper with the headline: *Strange burglary in Paris*. Famous actress Anna Bella has costume jewellery stolen.

Dix-septième unité

avez-vous compris? (p.250) **1** Le camion de déménagement va arriver à deux heures. **2** Chantal va emprunter la voiture de Laurent. **3** Chantal va arriver à l'appartement avant les déménageurs. **4** Dans l'appartement, il y a une salle de séjour. **5** Il y a une chambre, une cuisine et une petite salle de bain. **6** La salle de séjour donne sur un parc. **7** Sa chambre est de taille moyenne. **8** Chantal range ses vêtements dans l'armoire normande. **9** Dans la cuisine ils vont mettre la table, les tabourets et le vaisselier.

à vous! (p.250) **Salle de séjour:** une table, quatre chaises, deux fauteuils, un canapé, un buffet; **Chambre:** un lit, une commode, une table de nuit, une armoire; **Cuisine:** une table de cuisine, des tabourets, un vaisselier, un frigidaire.

avez-vous compris? (p.252) **1** Non. **2** Non. **3** Non. **4** Oui. **5** Non, seulement un frigo. **6** L'armoire normande. Elle est trop grande. **7** Il est tard. **8** Sur le palier. **9** Oui. Elle n'a que des gros billets. **10** Laurent. **11** Au dernier étage. **12** (*Suggested answers*) Je ne sais pas! / Elle va la vendre. / Elle va la laisser sur le palier. / Elle va la mettre dans la salle de séjour.

avez-vous compris? (p.254) You should have ticked: **1** une cuillère, **2** une tasse, **3** une poêle, **4** un placard, **5** une nappe, **6** un tire-bouchon, **7** dans un tiroir.

EXERCICES **A** (*Suggested answers*) **1** Il y a un lit, deux tables de nuit, une commode et une armoire. **2** Elle donne sur la rue. **3** Elle est de taille moyenne. **4** Il y a une table, deux tabourets, un frigidaire, une machine à laver et des placards. **5** Il y a un canapé, deux fauteuils, une télévision, une table et des chaises. **6** J'aime bien mon appartement parce qu'il est confortable. / Je n'aime pas mon appartement parce qu'il est trop petit. **B** (*Suggested answers*) **1** Je viens de rencontrer une amie. **2** Nous venons de prendre le train. **3** Elle vient de recevoir un cadeau. **4** Je viens de marcher sur les pieds d'une dame. **5** Ils viennent d'avoir un bébé. **6** Il vient de me demander d'aller au cinéma. **7** Tu viens de perdre tout ton argent au casino. **8** Vous venez d'arriver à l'hôtel. **C 1** j, **2** i, **3** c, **4** a, **5** h, **6** e, **7** g, **8** d, **9** f, **10** b. **D 1** f, **2** h, **3** b, **4** a, **5** d, **6** g, **7** e, **8** c. **E 1** e la, **2** h le, **3** j le, **4** g la, **5** d les, **6** a la, **7** b la, **8** c le, **9** f les, **10** i le. **F 1** le, **2** la, **3** la, **4** les, **5** le, **6** les, **7** les, **8** la.

écoutez bien! **1** The only one available was in the corner, not by the window as Mrs Brède wanted. **2** It was dirty. **3** It was cracked. **4** The service was slow. **5** The chicken was cold. **6** He didn't have one. **7** She didn't have one. **8** It was the bill of a couple celebrating their wedding anniversary with caviar and champagne.

Dix-huitième unité

 avez-vous compris? (p.262) **1** vrai, **2** faux, **3** vrai, **4** faux, **5** vrai, **6** vrai.

avez-vous compris? (p.263)   **1** vrai, **2** vrai, **3** vrai,
4 faux, **5** faux.

 à vous! (p.263)   **1** pêcheur, **2** infirmier / infirmière ou
médecin, **3** acteur / actrice ou chanteur / chanteuse.

 avez-vous compris? (p.267)   **1** faux, **2** faux, **3** faux,
4 vrai.

 avez-vous compris? (p.267)   **1** faux, **2** vrai, **3** vrai,
4 vrai, **5** faux.

 à vous! (p.268)   **1** e, **2** g, **3** b, **4** f, **5** a, **6** c, **7** d.

 avez-vous compris? (p.269)   **1** Édith, **2** Josée,
3 Josée, **4** Édith, **5** Josée, **6** Édith, **7** Josée, **8** Édith, **9** Josée.

EXERCICES   **A 1** Ils se dépêchent toujours.
2 Quelquefois ils ne se lavent pas! **3** Damien a seize ans et Irène a
quatorze ans. **4** Damien se rase, et il se dispute toujours avec sa sœur!
B (*Suggested answer*) Le samedi, nous ne nous levons pas de bonne
heure. Nous prenons un petit déjeuner à l'anglaise, puis nous nous
lavons et nous nous habillons. En général, ma femme se lave les
cheveux, et moi, je ne me rase pas. Ma femme fait les lits et la vaisselle.
Moi, je passe l'aspirateur. Quelquefois, je bricole ou je fais du jardinage.
L'après-midi, nous allons en ville faire des courses. Si nous sortons le
soir, nous nous changeons. Ma femme se maquille et je me rase. Quand

nous rentrons tard, nous nous couchons et nous nous endormons tout de suite. Et le dimanche matin, nous nous réveillons très tard!
C 1 c, **2** f, **3** d, **4** h, **5** a, **6** e, **7** g, **8** b.   **D 1** lui, **2** lui, **3** leur, **4** lui, **5** leur.
E 1 y, **2** en, **3** en, **4** y, **5** en, **6** y, **7** en, **8** en, **9** y, **10** en.

écoutez bien!   **2** s'appeler, **9** se coucher, **1** s'habiller, **3** se lever, **10** se raser, **4** se brosser les dents, **5** s'endormir, **8** se réveiller, **7** se maquiller, **6** se laver.

Faites le point! (unités 16–18)

1 a sort, **b** rougissons, **c** finissez, **d** choisissent, **e** dors. **2 a** vient, **b** vais, **c** revenons, **d** vont, **e** viennent, **f** vas, **g** venons, **h** va, **i** venez, **j** allons. **3 a** Elle vient vient de partir. **b** Nous venons de manger. **c** Vous venez d'être malade. **d** Ils viennent de finir la bouteille. **e** Je viens de perdre mon porte-monnaie. **4 a** appelez-vous; **b** m'appelle, me lève, me lave; **c** m'appelle, me lève, me brosse les cheveux, me maquille; **d** appelons, levons, rasons, habillons; **e** vous couchez, m'endors; **f** me change, me brosse. **5 a** vous vous changez, **b** je ne me maquille pas, **c** coiffez-vous / vous coiffez, **d** je me lave, je me couche. **6 a** l', **b** la, **c** l', **d** les, **e** le. **7 a** lui, **b** lui, **c** leur, **d** lui, **e** leur. **8 a** y, **b** en, **c** en, **d** en, **e** y, **f** en, **g** y, **h** en. **9 a** un manteau, **b** un ouvre-boîte, **c** le palais, **d** une chaussure. **10 a** (v), **b** (vi), **c** (vii), **d** (i), **e** (x), **f** (ix), **g** (iii), **h** (viii), **i** (iv), **j** (ii).

Dix-neuvième unité

avez-vous compris? (p.282)   Stay at home, watch TV / video or a DVD, telephone, have a bath or shower, listen to the radio or music, read, use the computer, do some sport, visit friends, play Scrabble / chess, etc. invite friends, eat out, play cards, do some kind of housework, work, write a letter/e-mail, go to the cinema, the theatre or a concert.

à vous! (p.282) **1 Quarante** pour **cent** ont lu. **2** Treize pour cent ont **joué** aux **cartes**. **3 Trente** et **un** pour cent ont **fait** du sport. **4** Soixante-quatorze **pour cent** ont **téléphoné**. **5 Dix pour cent** ont travaillé. **6** Quarante-trois pour cent ont **écouté** la **radio** ou de la **musique**. **7** Vingt pour cent sont allés **chez des amis**. **8** Trente-huit pour cent ont utilisé **l'ordinateur**. **9 Quinze pour cent** ont mangé **au restaurant**. **10** Soixante-six **pour cent** ont **pris** un bain ou une douche. **11 Huit pour cent** ont écrit une lettre. **12 Quatre-vingt-cinq** pour cent sont restés **à la maison**.

avez-vous compris? (p.283) **1** faux, **2** vrai, **3** vrai, **4** faux, **5** vrai, **6** vrai, **7** vrai, **8** vrai, **9** faux, **10** faux. **1** Lundi matin je suis allée chez le dentiste. **4** Jeudi j'ai fait le ménage. **9** Samedi soir je suis allée au restaurant. **10** Dimanche je suis allée à la piscine.

EXERCICES   **A 1** h, **2** d, **3** a, **4** f, **5** g, **6** b, **7** e, **8** c.
B 1 J'ai bavardé. **2** J'ai chanté. **3** J'ai joué aux cartes. **4** J'ai dansé. **5** J'ai fait du ski. **6** J'ai fait la cuisine. **7** J'ai lu. **8** J'ai fait du vélo. **9** J'ai tricoté.

10 J'ai mangé une pomme. **11** J'ai fait mes devoirs. **12** J'ai joué de la trompette. **C 1** Vous avez bavardé? / Avez-vous bavardé? **2** Vous avez chanté? / Avez-vous chanté? **3** Vous avez joué aux cartes? / Avez-vous joué aux cartes? **4** Vous avez dansé? / Avez-vous dansé? **5** Vous avez fait du ski? / Avez-vous fait du ski? **6** Vous avez fait la cuisine? Avez-vous fait la cuisine? **7** Vous avez lu? / Avez-vous lu? **8** Vous avez fait du vélo? / Avez-vous fait du vélo? **9** Vous avez tricoté? / Avez-vous tricoté? **10** Vous avez mangé une pomme? / Avez-vous mangé une pomme? **11** Vous avez fait vos devoirs? / Avez-vous fait vos devoirs? **12** Vous avez joué de la trompette? / Avez-vous joué de la trompette? **D** Cher / Chère … J'ai fait bon voyage. Il ne fait pas beau et je ne suis pas allé(e) à la plage. Lundi dernier, j'ai visité un château. Hier je suis resté(e) à l'hôtel. Le soir, j'ai mangé dans un petit restaurant du port, puis, je suis allé(e) au cinéma. Amitiés / Amicalement, **E 1** J'ai mangé du couscous. **2** Je suis allé(e) en Espagne. **3** J'ai lu un magazine. **4** J'ai pris mon bain à huit heures. **5** J'ai écrit une lettre à mon ami allemand. **6** Je suis allé(e) au cinéma lundi dernier. **7** Je n'ai pas joué avec Kasparov! **8** J'ai regardé une émission sur la Chine à la télé. **9** J'ai invité mon oncle et ma tante. **10** Je suis allé(e) à l'opéra la semaine dernière.

écoutez bien! **When they went** The children: yesterday; Bernard: last Saturday; Annette: last weekend; Monsieur Roquand: last week; Madame Orgerit: Tuesday evening. **Where they went** The children: library; Bernard: at friends'; Annette: London; Monsieur Roquand: the Alps; Madame Orgerit: stayed at home. **What they did** The children: read comic strips; Bernard: had a Chinese meal; Annette: visited the Tower, bought clothes; Monsieur Roquand: went skiing; Madame Orgerit: watched the news and an American film on T.V.

Vingtième unité

avez-vous compris? (p.288)   un pied (*foot*), la taille (*waist*), le dos (*back*), le cou (*neck*) were not mentioned.

avez-vous compris? (p.291)   **1** h, **2** f, **3** j, **4** a, **5** i, **6** b, **7** d, **8** c, **9** e, **10** g.

avez-vous compris? (p.293)   **1** vrai, **2** faux, **3** faux, **4** vrai, **5** faux, **6** vrai, **7** vrai, **8** faux, **9** faux, **10** vrai.

avez-vous compris? (p.294)   You should have ticked: **1** à la gorge, **2** le sirop à la banane, **3** mal à la tête, **4** les coups de soleil, **5** une crème, **6** a mal au cœur, **7** le mal de mer, **8** contre l'indigestion.

à vous! (p.295)   **1** à la tête, **2** aux dents, **3** au pied, **4** au ventre, **5** aux genoux, **6** au dos, **7** au cœur, **8** à la gorge, **9** aux oreilles, **10** aux yeux.

EXERCICES   **A 1** Levez-vous! **2** Mettez les mains sur les hanches! **3** Penchez-vous à droite, puis à gauche! **4** Tendez les bras! **5** Levez la jambe droite, puis la gauche! **6** Ralentissez. **7** Pliez légèrement les genoux! **8** Touchez vos pieds! **9** Asseyez-vous! **10** Tournez la tête à droite, puis à gauche! **11** Couchez-vous sur le dos! **12** Levez la jambe gauche puis baissez-la! **13** N'oubliez pas de respirer. **14** Fermez les yeux! **15** Soufflez par la bouche! **B 1** e, **2** f, **3** a, **4** c,

5 d, **6** b. **C 1** Docteur, j'ai mal partout! **2** Oui, et j'ai aussi mal à la gorge.
3 Je ne sais pas. Je n'ai pas pris ma température. **4** J'ai aussi mal au
ventre. **5** Non, mais j'ai mal au cœur. **6** Je préfère des comprimés.

écoutez bien! Première Partie 2, 6, 1, 5, 9, 7, 3, 10, 8, 4.
Deuxième Partie 1 Car sickness, pills. **2** Headache, aspirin. **3** Mosquito
bites, protective cream. **4** Cough / sore throat, suppositories.
5 Temperature, stay in bed / drink a lot of water. **6** Sunburn, soothing
lotion. **7** Backache, rest / take tablets morning, lunchtime and evening.
8 Stop smoking, herbal cigarettes.

Vingt et unième unité

avez-vous compris? (p.301) Gérard: 4. Sylviane: 6.

avez-vous compris? (p.305) Sylviane: 1, 3, 4, 6, 8.
Gérard: 2, 5, 7.

à vous! (p.305) Est-ce que je peux … Est-ce qu'on
peut … **1** louer une voiture? **2** réserver une chambre? **3** avoir un plan
de la ville? **4** avoir une carte de la région? **5** téléphoner à la gare?
6 visiter un château ou un musée? **7** jouer au golf ou au tennis dans la
région? **8** nager / faire de la natation? **9** faire des promenades?
10 avoir une liste des terrains de camping?

avez-vous compris? (p.307) **1** Pour les vacances.
2 Un maillot de bain deux pièces. **3** Un régime très sévère. **4** Parce que
son mari est boulanger-pâtissier. **5** Les vacances.

à vous! (p.307) **1** d, **2** f, **3** h, **4** b, **5** g, **6** a, **7** e, **8** c.

 avez-vous compris? (p.308) You should have ticked:
1 est allée en Italie. **2** veut. **3** voisins. **4** troisième. **5** régulièrement.
6 un peu. **7** supérette. **8** une heure.

avez-vous compris? (p.309) Chantal goes to an
evening class to learn English. She has a boyfriend called Laurent who
works in a bank. She has been going out with him for about 3 months.
They want to go on holiday together, somewhere in France, but they
have not decided where to go yet.

à vous! (p.310) **1** Vous connaissez. **2** Vous savez. **3** Vous
savez. **4** Vous connaissez. **5** Vous savez. **6** Vous savez. **7** Vous
connaissez. **8** Vous connaissez. **9** Vous savez. **10** Vous connaissez.
11 Vous savez. **12** Vous savez.

EXERCICES **A 1** veux, **2** voulons, **3** veut, **4** voulez,
5 veux, **6** veulent. **B 1** devez, **2** peut, **3** devez, **4** dois, **5** devons,
6 pouvez. **C** Est-ce qu'on peut … **1** manger? **2** téléphoner? **3** prendre
des photos? **4** fumer? **5** payer avec une carte de crédit? **6** stationner?
7 prendre une douche? **8** camper / faire du camping? **D 1** connais,
2 connaissez, **3** connaissez, **4** connais, **5** sais, **6** savez. **E** 5, 8, 2, 4, 6, 1,
3, 7, 9. **F 2** L'autruche ne peut pas voler. **3** Il ne sait pas nager. **4** Le chien

ne peut pas mordre. **5** Le bébé ne veut pas manger. **6** Il ne sait pas danser. **7** L'âne ne veut pas avancer. **8** Ils ne peuvent pas parler.

écoutez bien! Première partie 1 dix-huit, **2** grande, **3** trente-deux, **4** brune, **5** longs, **6** raides, **7** les yeux, **8** des lunettes, **9** un pantalon, **10** une veste, **11** un sac, **12** valise, **13** rendez-vous.
Deuxième partie 1 f, **2** d, **3** h, **4** c, **5** a, **6** g, **7** e, **8** b.
Troisième partie 1 c, **2** e, **3** a, **4** b, **5** f, **6** d.

Faites le point! (unités 19–21)

1 a Les cheveux, **b** les yeux, **c** un œil, **d** une oreille, **e** le nez, **f** la bouche, **g** les dents, **h** le cou, **i** la tête. **2 a** Une épaule, **b** un bras, **c** une main, **d** le dos, **e** le ventre, **f** la taille, **g** les genoux, **h** une jambe, **i** un pied.
3 a Touchez vos pieds mais pliez les genoux. **b** Couchez-vous sur le dos.
c Mettez les mains sur les hanches. **d** Fermez les yeux. **e** Tournez la tête à droite puis à gauche. **f** N'oubliez pas de respirer par le nez. **4 a** j'ai fait, **b** j'ai écouté, **c** j'ai lu, **d** j'ai regardé, **e** je suis allée, **f** j'ai mangé.
5 a (vi), **b** (v), **c** (vii), **d** (ii), **e** (i), **f** (viii), **g** (iv), **h** (iii). **6 a** vous **devez**, **b** je ne **veux** pas, **c** vous **devez**, **d** je **dois**, **e** je **peux**, **f** **voulez**-vous.
7 a **connaissez**-vous, **b** **savez**-vous, **c** je **connais**, **d** je ne **sais** pas.
8 a (iii), **b** (v), **c** (iv), **d** (vi), **e** (i), **f** (ii).

Écoutez bien! – tape transcripts

Première unité

Première partie 1 Je suis de Toulouse. **2** Nous sommes de Lille.
3 Je suis de Nice en Provence. **4** Je suis de Cherbourg en Normandie.
5 Je suis de Dijon en Bourgogne. **6** Nous sommes de Bastia en Corse.
7 Je suis de Vichy. **8** Nous sommes de Rennes en Bretagne. **9** Je suis de
Limoges. **10** Nous sommes de Grenoble.
Deuxième partie 1 a Il est français. / **b** Il est français / **c** Elle est
française. **2 a** Il est anglais. / **b** Il est anglais. / **c** Elle est anglaise.
3 a Vous êtes écossaise. / **b** Vous êtes écossais. / **c** Vous êtes écossais.
4 a Il est de Rouen. / **b** Elle est de Rouen. / **c** Il est de Rouen.
5 a Bonjour mademoiselle. / **b** Bonjour madame. / **c** Bonjour madame.
6 a Il est américian. / **b** Ils sont américains. / **c** Il est américain.
7 a Je suis de Paris. / **b** Je suis de Paris. / **c** Nous sommes de Paris.
8 a Elle est espagnole. / **b** Il est espagnol. / **c** Il est espagnol.

Deuxième unité

1 – Bonjour, monsieur. Comment vous appelez-vous?
– Je m'appelle Henri. Et vous mademoiselle?
– Moi, je m'appelle Jeanne.
2 – D'où êtes-vous madame?
– Je suis de Bastia, c'est en Corse. Et vous?
– Je suis anglais, de Londres.

3 – Qui est-ce?

– Je ne sais pas!

– Est-ce que c'est le guide?

– Je ne sais pas!

4 – Quelle est votre situation de famille?

– Je suis célibataire. Et vous?

– Moi aussi, mais j'ai un petit ami allemand.

5 – Quel est votre métier, monsieur?

– Je suis pêcheur.

– En France?

– Oui, en Bretagne. Et vous?

– Moi, je suis ouvrier dans une usine.

6 – Où travaillez-vous, madame?

– Je travaille dans un hôpital.

– Ah, vous êtes infirmière?

– Non, je ne suis pas infirmière, je suis médecin.

Troisième unité

Première partie

Table numéro un

Client S'il vous plaît, monsieur! Ça fait combien?

Serveur Alors… Deux cafés et un grand crème, ça fait onze euros, messieurs-dames.

Table numéro 2

Client Pardon monsieur, je vous dois combien?

Serveur   Voyons… un coca, un jus d'orange, un citron pressé et une bière. Alors ça fait quatorze euros, s'il vous plaît.

Table numéro trois

Client   Je vous dois combien, monsieur?

Serveur   Alors, nous avons deux cognacs, trois kirs, deux vins blancs et deux vins rouges. Ça fait cinquante euros exactement.

Table numéro quatre

Cliente   On vous doit combien, s'il vous plaît?

Serveur   Deux cafés, deux jus d'orange, une bière pression et un citron pressé, ça vous fait dix-neuf euros en tout.

Table numéro cinq

Client   Monsieur! L'addition, s'il vous plaît!

Serveur   Tout de suite, monsieur… Alors, un panaché à trois euros, une bière pression à trois euros cinquante et deux schweppes, ça vous fait douze euros cinquante, monsieur.

Deuxième partie

Mme Bigger   Vous avez une maison, monsieur Lepetit?

M. Lepetit   Non, j'ai seulement un petit appartement à Paris. Et vous?

Mme Bigger   Moi, j'ai un appartement à New York – il est immense – une grande maison en Floride et un ranch au Texas.

M. Lepetit   Vous avez des enfants?

Mme Bigger   Non, je n'ai pas d'enfants. Je déteste les enfants!

M. Lepetit   Moi, j'ai quatre enfants, un chien, deux chats, des poissons rouges…

Mme Bigger   Moi, je déteste les animaux! Je n'ai pas d'animal familier, mais j'ai plusieurs voitures!

M. Lepetit	Plusieurs voitures?
Mme Bigger	Oui, j'en ai trois. Une petite voiture française à New York, c'est très pratique, une énorme voiture américaine en Floride – elle est très confortable – et une jeep au Texas.
M. Lepetit	Vous avez un avion, un bateau aussi peut-être?
Mme Bigger	Mon mari a un hélicoptère, et nous avons un yacht magnifique en Méditerranée.
M. Lepetit	Moi, j'ai un vélo.
Mme Bigger	Mon mari aussi a un vélo, mais moi, je déteste le sport!

Quatrième unité

L'alphabet français: A, B, C, D, E, F, G, H, I, J, K, L, M, N, O, P, Q, R, S, T, U, V, W, X, Y, Z.

Première partie

Réceptionniste	Allô, hôtel Europa, j'écoute!
Client	Allô! Bonjour madame. Je voudrais réserver une chambre.
Réceptionniste	Oui monsieur, pour combien de personnes?
Client	Pour deux personnes, pour moi et pour ma femme.
Réceptionniste	Et c'est pour combien de nuits?
Client	Une seulement, le quatorze mai.
Réceptionniste	Vous préférez avec salle de bain ou avec douche?
Client	Je ne sais pas!
Réceptionniste	Nous avons une chambre avec douche qui fait 100 euros.
Client	Combien?

Réceptionniste	Cent euros et le petit déjeuner fait 15 euros par personne.
Client	Il y a un restaurant?
Réceptionniste	Non, monsieur, je regrette, mais il y en a d'excellents dans la région.
Client	Ça va, je la prends.
Réceptionniste	Quel est votre nom, monsieur?
Client	Martineau, M–A–R–T–I–N–E–A–U.

Deuxième partie 1 Y–I–O–A–U–H–R–W–J– X–K–V–E–T–G.
2 Lyon: L-Y-O-N, Ajaccio: A-J-A-2-C-I-O, Tours: T-O-U-R, Strasbourg: S-T-R-A-S-B-O-U-R-G, Bordeaux: B-O-R-D-A-U-X, Quimper: Q-U-I-M-P-E-R.

Cinquième unité

1 – Vous avez choisi, madame?
 – Oui, je voudrais du poulet rôti avec des frites, s'il vous plaît.
2 – Que prenez-vous au petit déjeuner, monsieur?
 – Je mange des croissants ou du pain grillé.
3 – Qu'est-ce qu'il y a comme dessert?
 – Aujourd'hui, c'est de la salade de fruits.
4 – Que prenez-vous au petit déjeuner les enfants?
 – On boit du chocolat chaud ou du lait.
5 – Que prendrez-vous pour commencer?
 – Je voudrais de la soupe aux champignons.

6 – Qu'est-ce qu'il y a comme fruits aujourd'hui?

– Aujourd'hui il y a des poires et des bananes.

7 – Le beurre est dans le frigidaire?

– Oui, bien sûr!

– Et la confiture de fraise?

– Désolée, je ne sais pas!

8 – Est-ce que vous avez des jus de fruits?

– Oui, orange ou pamplemousse?

– Pamplemousse, s'il vous plaît.

9 – Pour commencer, je voudrais une soupe de tomates.

– Je suis désolé, il n'y a pas de soupe aujourd'hui.

10 – Tu as soif Antoine?

– Oui, je voudrais une bière.

11 – S'il vous plaît!

– Oui, monsieur.

– Je voudrais de la moutarde avec ma viande froide.

– Tout de suite, monsieur.

12 – Je voudrais une baguette, s'il vous plaît.

– Je suis désolé, il n'y a plus de pain.

13 – Qu'est-ce que vous avez comme sandwichs?

– Alors, aujourd'hui, il y a des sandwichs au jambon et des sandwichs au fromage.

14 – Vous préférez le thé ou le café, Sylvie?

– Je préfère le thé-citron.

15 – Vous avez faim?

– Oui, je voudrais du poisson et des frites.

Sixième unité

Première partie

1 – Quel âge ont Charlotte et Juliette?

  – Charlotte a huit ans et Juliette a seize ans.

2 – Quel âge avez-vous?

  – J'ai dix-sept ans, et mon frère a quatorze ans.

3 – Quel âge a le chat d'Henri?

  – Il a seulement six mois.

4 – Marie a de la chance!

  – Pourquoi?

  – Elle n'a pas de sœurs!

5 – Vous avez faim les enfants?

  – Ah non, maman, mais nous avons soif!

6 – Chantal, tu as froid dans le jardin?

  – Ah non, papa! En fait, j'ai chaud.

Deuxième partie

1 – J'ai perdu mes lunettes!

  – Elles sont sur le bureau, entre la lampe et le magazine.

2 – Où est mon stylo?

  – Dans le tiroir de la table de nuit.

3 – J'ai perdu mon parapluie!

  – Il est par terre, devant le radiateur.

4 – Mes clés! J'ai perdu mes clés!

  – Les clés de la maison?

  – Non, les clés de la voiture!

  – Elles sont dans votre sac peut-être?

5 – Fifi! Fifi! Où est passée la chienne?
– Elle a peur! Elle est sans doute dans votre chambre, sous le lit.

Septième unité

Première partie

1 – Excusez-moi, je cherche une boulangerie. Il y en a une par ici?
– Oui bien sûr, à 150 mètres, sur votre gauche.

2 – Pardon monsieur, est-ce que la gare est loin d'ici?
– C'est à environ 15 minutes. Vous avez une grosse valise, prenez le bus, le numéro 12.

3 – Pour aller au centre commercial, s'il vous plaît?
– Alors, continuez tout droit, aux feux rouges tournez à gauche, puis prenez la deuxième à droite.
– Oh là là! C'est loin?
– Non, c'est seulement à 3 kilomètres.

4 – Pardon monsieur, le château, c'est loin d'ici?
– Vous êtes en voiture j'espère, c'est à 20 kilomètres.

5 – Je cherche des toilettes, c'est urgent!
– Il y a des toilettes au bout de la rue.
– C'est loin?
– C'est à 5 minutes.
– Merci, merci!

6 – Pardon, mademoiselle, où est la bibliothèque, s'il vous plaît?
– Je suis désolée monsieur, je ne suis pas d'ici, je ne sais pas!

Deuxième partie

1 – Pardon, monsieur l'agent, pour aller à la poste, s'il vous plaît?
  – C'est facile. Prenez la deuxième rue à gauche.
2 – Je cherche la piscine.
  – Traversez la rue. La piscine est juste en face.
3 – Pardon, monsieur l'agent, où est le commissariat de police?
  – Alors, vous prenez la première à droite, puis la deuxième à gauche.
4 – Il y a un supermarché par ici?
  – Oui, vous continuez jusqu'aux feux, puis vous prenez la deuxième à droite.
5 – Je cherche une pharmacie.
  – Vous traversez le pont et vous prenez la première à droite.
  – Merci beaucoup. Au revoir, monsieur l'agent.
6 – Pour aller au château, s'il vous plaît?
  – Alors, vous continuez tout droit, puis vous tournez à gauche.

Huitième unité

1 – Pardon messieurs–dames. Où habitez-vous?
  – Nous habitons dans une petite maison en banlieue.
2 – Éric et Bernard travaillent dans une usine. Vous aussi?
  – Non, moi je ne travaille pas!
3 – Sophie préfère la danse ou la musique?
  – La musique. Elle joue du piano et elle chante dans une chorale.
4 – Vous parlez allemand?
  – Non, mais j'étudie l'espagnol.
5 – Les enfants aiment l'anglais?

– Oui, ils adorent écouter de la musique anglaise et regarder des films américains.

6 – Qu'est-ce que tu achètes?

– Du poisson. J'en mange souvent. J'adore ça!

Neuvième unité

1 – Où est ton frère?

– Dans le jardin, avec des amis.

– Qu'est-ce qu'ils font?

– Ils jouent au football.

2 – Sophie, où es-tu?

– Je suis au salon, maman.

– Qu'est-ce que tu fais?

– Je regarde la télé.

3 – Où sont tes beaux-parents?

– Ils sont en vacances en ce moment.

– Ah bon, où ça? En France?

– Oui, ils sont en Bretagne.

4 – Allô!

– Allô! C'est Nicole?

– Oui!

– Je voudrais parler à ton père. Il est à la maison?

– Ah non, il travaille aujourd'hui, il est au bureau.

5 – Allô!

– Allô, c'est Gilles! Je voudrais parler à Françoise.

– Impossible, ma sœur est dans la salle de bain.

– Qu'est-ce qu'elle fait?

– Elle prend une douche.

6 – Philippe, qu'est-ce qu'elle fait ta grand-mère?

– Elle fait le ménage.

– Où est-elle?

– Elle est dans la salle à manger maintenant.

7 – Qu'est-ce que vous faites dans la cuisine, les enfants?

– Nous avons faim maman; nous préparons des sandwichs.

Dixième unité

– Pardon, monsieur, je voudrais vous poser quelques questions.

– D'accord, je ne suis pas pressé aujourd'hui!

– Est-ce que vous êtes sportif?

– Quand il fait beau je fais du vélo, l'hiver je fais du ski et, de temps en temps, je vais à la piscine.

– Piscine … de temps en temps. Vous aimez lire le journal?

– Non, je lis rarement le journal.

– Rarement…Vous préférez le cinéma ou le théâtre?

– Je préfère le cinéma, je vais souvent au cinéma.

– Cinéma…souvent. Est-ce que vous aimez faire la cuisine?

– J'aime bien faire la cuisine pendant le week-end, le samedi soir par exemple, quand nous avons des amis à dîner.

– Et est-ce que vous faites aussi la vaisselle?

– Je déteste faire la vaisselle, mais je la fais tous les soirs!

– Vaisselle…tous les soirs. Où est-ce que vous allez en vacances?

– Quelquefois, nous allons à la montagne, mais les enfants préfèrent

aller au bord de la mer.
– Quelquefois…montagne. Est-ce que vous allez souvent à l'étranger?
– Je vais régulièrement en Allemagne pour mon travail.
– Régulièrement…Aimez-vous le jardinage?
– Oui, beaucoup. Nous avons un petit jardin et en général, je fais le jardinage le dimanche.
– Jardinage…Vous aimez jouer aux cartes?
– Oui, j'adore jouer aux cartes. Je joue au bridge avec des amis une fois par semaine.
– Bien…Et la dernière question: Est-ce que vous aimez aller à la pêche?
– Non, je ne vais jamais à la pêche. Je déteste le poisson!

Onzième unité

Première partie

Enquêteur Pardon, madame. J'aimerais vous poser quelques questions sur votre emploi du temps. Vous n'êtes pas trop pressée, j'espère.

Femme Non, ça va. C'est mon heure de déjeuner.

Enquêteur Combien de temps avez-vous pour déjeuner?

Femme De midi à une heure. Quand il fait beau, comme aujourd'hui, je mange un sandwich et je fais une petite promenade. Sinon, je mange à la cantine.

Enquêteur Vous faites des courses pendant votre heure de déjeuner?

Femme Quelquefois.

Enquêteur Allez-vous souvent au supermarché?

Femme J'y vais une fois par semaine, ça suffit!

Enquêteur Quel jour y allez-vous?

Femme En général, le samedi. Mais je déteste ça. Je préfère aller au marché avec mon mari le dimanche matin.

Enquêteur À quelle heure?

Femme Nous quittons la maison à dix heures, dix heures et quart et nous rentrons vers midi.

Enquêteur Vous n'allez pas à la messe le dimanche?

Femme Je suis catholique, mais je n'y vais pas souvent. À Noël et à Pâques, bien sûr, et de temps en temps le dimanche, à la messe de six heures.

Enquêteur Du matin?

Femme Non, du soir!

Enquêteur Vous préférez sans doute regarder la télé!

Femme Oui, j'aime beaucoup la télévision.

Enquêteur Vous la regardez beaucoup?

Femme Oui, tous les soirs.

Enquêteur À quelle heure?

Femme À partir de huit heures jusqu'à minuit, minuit et demi. Malheureusement, c'est le soir tard qu'il y a les émissions les plus intéressantes!

Enquêteur Vous dînez à quelle heure?

Femme Nous mangeons à sept heures et demie tous les jours.

Enquêteur Vous rentrez du travail à quelle heure?

Femme Je suis chez moi vers six heures.

Enquêteur Et vous commencez à quelle heure?

Femme J'ai de la chance, je commence seulement à neuf heures du matin.

Enquêteur Parlons maintenant de votre …

Deuxième partie

Vendeuse Bonjour, monsieur, vous désirez?

Homme Je ne sais pas exactement. Je cherche un cadeau pour des amis.

Vendeuse Un souvenir d'Alsace?

Homme C'est une bonne idée!

Vendeuse Ce joli vase par exemple, il fait 22 euros.

Homme Et ce livre sur l'Alsace?

Vendeuse Il y a des photos splendides dedans. Il coûte 61 euros.

Homme 61 euros, c'est cher!

Vendeuse Pourquoi pas une bouteille de Mirabelle, c'est une spécialité de la région, pour 38 euros.

Homme Ils n'aiment pas l'alcool.

Vendeuse Alors, des chocolats, des bonbons? Cette belle boîte de chocolats fait 25 euros.

Homme Et le paquet de bonbons?

Vendeuse 4 euros 50.

Homme Je préfère quelque chose de plus personnel.

Vendeuse Un stylo peut-être? Voilà un stylo très élégant pour 26 euros.

Homme Ils adorent la musique. Vous avez des CD?

Vendeuse Bien sûr! Ce CD de musique folklorique par exemple fait 30 euros.

Homme Hmm…non, je vais prendre le stylo pour Paul et un bouquet de fleurs séchées pour Paulette.

Vendeuse Très bien, monsieur. Alors, 26 euros pour le stylo, et 19 euros pour les fleurs. Ça vous fait 45 euros en tout.

Douzième unité

Première partie: à la gare

Attention, attention! Changements d'horaires des TGV en partance de la gare de Lyon aujourd'hui. TGV à destination d'Annecy, départ sept heures vingt-quatre, arrivée dix heures cinquante-neuf. TGV à destination de Lausanne, départ douze heures vingt-cinq, arrivée seize heures zéro six. TGV à destination de Dijon, départ quatorze heures vingt, arrivée quinze heures cinquante-six. TGV à destination de Macon, départ quatorze heures trente-deux, arrivée seize heures treize. TGV à destination de Genève, départ dix-sept heures quarante-deux, arrivée vingt et une heures treize. TGV à destination de Berne, départ dix-huit heures zéro six, arrivée vingt-deux heures trente-sept.

Deuxième partie: à la radio

Chers auditeurs, bonjour. Vous écoutez France-Radio. Dans quelques instants, les informations de midi, mais avant, permettez–moi de vous rappeler quelques émissions à ne pas manquer cette semaine. Très important, si vous allez travailler en voiture; informez-vous sur l'état de la circulation, et détendez-vous, en musique, dans les embouteillages avec 'la route en chansons', tous les matins, du lundi au vendredi, de six heures à dix heures. Ce soir, à 21h 30, ne manquez surtout pas le résultat de notre grande enquête nationale sur le cinéma: Qui va au cinéma? Quels films les Français préfèrent-ils? Demain après-midi, restez à l'écoute de 'Jacqueline et Compagnie', de 14 à 16 heures, pour l'invitée spéciale de Jacqueline, la jeune journaliste Véronique Tilon, qui parlera de ses extraordinaires aventures en Afrique. Et samedi après-midi, à partir de 15 heures, le hit-parade, le rendez-vous de nos jeunes auditeurs, animé comme d'habitude par Léo, leur disque-jockey favori. Il est midi, voici donc Info-Déjeuner, présenté aujourd'hui par Didier Gallet.

Treizième unité

avez-vous compris? (p.193) **Josée** J'aime beaucoup le chemisier, mais je déteste la jupe… Je n'aime pas le tailleur, mais le pull-over en mohair me plaît beaucoup… J'adore la petite veste en fourrure et j'aime bien la robe aussi… J'aime assez l'imperméable et le pantalon, mais je n'aime pas du tout le corsage à fleurs… je n'aime pas le manteau de tweed… J'aime beaucoup la robe du soir.

à vous! (p.198) **Lucien** Regarde, Josée. Le smoking, la chemise à jabot de dentelle et le nœud papillon. C'est très chic!… J'adore le blouson à carreaux… Je voudrais la chemise à rayures, la rose et blanche, et la cravate en soie bordeaux…J'aime beaucoup le costume en polyester bleu marine…Et j'ai besoin d'un jean aussi… Mais je n'ai pas besoin d'un pardessus. C'est beaucoup trop chaud pour la Martinique!

Vendeuse	Bonjour, monsieur. Vous désirez?
François	Je voudrais faire un cadeau à ma femme…Je ne sais pas…euh, une chemise de nuit peut-être.
Vendeuse	Oui, monsieur, nous avons de très jolies chemises de nuit. Vous la voulez longue ou courte?

François	Longue, avec de la dentelle.
Vendeuse	Bien sûr, monsieur. Et quelle est la taille de votre femme?
François	Elle prend du quarante-deux.
Vendeuse	Bon. Nous avons ce très joli modèle en blanc ou en champagne. Voici un autre modèle qui existe en bleu ou en rose. Ou bien cette chemise de nuit tout en dentelle noire, très décolletée.
François	La noire me plaît beaucoup. Elle coûte combien?
Vendeuse	Ce modèle fait 116 euros.
François	Oh là là, c'est beaucoup trop cher! C'est dommage. Et la blanche?
Vendeuse	Alors, la blanche fait 65 euros, monsieur.
François	Hmm…Et la bleue?
Vendeuse	Voyons, la bleue fait 54 euros.
François	C'est parfait, ma femme a les yeux bleus.
Vendeuse	Voulez-vous la robe de chambre assortie?
François	Non, merci. Seulement la chemise de nuit. Pouvez-vous me faire un joli paquet-cadeau?
Vendeuse	Mais bien sûr, monsieur.

Quatorzième unité

Au bureau des objets trouvés

1 – J'ai perdu mon parapluie.

– Où l'avez-vous perdu?

– Probablement dans le bus.

– Quel bus?

- Le numéro seize.
- Et comment est votre parapluie?
- Il est jaune et vert, à rayures.

2 - J'ai perdu ma valise. C'est une grosse valise bleue.
  - Où l'avez-vous perdue?
  - Je ne sais pas!
  - À la gare?
  - Impossible, j'ai voyagé en avion.
  - Dans un taxi?
  - Peut-être!
  - À l'hôtel?
  - Je ne sais pas où je l'ai perdue!

3 - J'ai perdu mon maillot de bain.
  - Comment est-il?
  - À fleurs.
  - De quelle couleur?
  - Rose et bleu.
  - Et où l'avez-vous perdu?
  - Probablement à la piscine.

4 - J'ai perdu mon sac à main.
  - Où ça?
  - Eh bien aujourd'hui j'ai visité le château et le musée.
  - Comment est votre sac?
  - Il est en cuir rouge. Dedans, il y a mon passeport, de l'argent, mes cartes de crédit, mes clés. C'est une véritable catastrophe!

5 - J'ai perdu Mimi!
  - Mimi?
  - Oui, mon Mimi, mon adorable petit Mimi!

– C'est votre…fils?

– Mais non, voyons, c'est mon chat.

– Ah bon! Comment est-il?

– Il est magnifique!

– Naturellement, mais donnez-moi des détails, âge, couleur…

– Il est noir et blanc, et il a seulement un an.

– Et où l'avez-vous perdu?

– Au marché, près du marchand de poisson.

Quinzième unité

1 – Les jumeaux vont au collège maintenant.

– Où vont-ils?

– Au collège Saint-Exupéry.

– C'est un bon collège, mais c'est loin de chez vous! Vous les emmenez en voiture?

– Non, c'est impossible, ils y vont en car.

2 – Ton mari va bien?

– Gilles va très bien, merci. Il travaille en ville maintenant. Ça lui plaît, mais la circulation est impossible.

– Il y va en voiture?

– Non, il prend le métro.

3 – Vous avez une voiture, Suzanne?

– Non, malheureusement!

– Comment allez-vous faire les courses, alors?

– En général j'y vais à pied, et une fois par semaine, pour aller au supermarché, j'appelle un taxi.

4 – Bernard voyage beaucoup pour son travail.

  – Il va à l'étranger?

  – Oui, très souvent, trop souvent même!

  – Comment voyage-t-il?

  – Il prend toujours l'avion parce que c'est plus rapide, mais il n'aime pas ça; il préfère le train.

5 – Comment va Alain?

  – Très bien, merci. Il est en vacances en ce moment.

  – Ah bon, en France?

  – Non, il est en Irlande. Il fait le tour de l'Irlande du sud en vélo, avec un groupe d'amis.

  – C'est une bonne idée ça!

6 – Vous travaillez, Sabine?

  – Oui, je suis représentante.

  – Vous voyagez beaucoup pour votre travail, alors!

  – Oui, je suis au bureau un ou deux jours par semaine seulement.

  – Ça ne vous dérange pas?

  – J'ai de la chance, j'ai une très bonne voiture, rapide et confortable, avec téléphone. Et puis, je descends toujours dans des hôtels de luxe.

Seizième unité

– Bonjour, monsieur. Quel est votre métier?

– Je suis serveur dans un petit restaurant à Rouen.

– Et où habitez-vous?

– J'habite à environ huit kilomètres du centre de la ville.

– Comment allez-vous au travail?

– J'y vais en moto, c'est plus pratique, car il y a toujours beaucoup de circulation.

– Même en hiver?

– Oui, mais quand il fait très mauvais, quand il neige par exemple, je prends la voiture.

– Vous partez de chez vous à quelle heure?

– En général, je pars à six heures, sauf le lundi parce que le restaurant est fermé.

– Vous travaillez pendant le week-end?

– Bien sûr. Il y a beaucoup de clients le samedi soir et le dimanche midi.

– Qu'est-ce qui vous plaît particulièrement dans votre métier?

– J'aime le contact direct avec les gens. Mes collègues sont très sympa.

– Et les clients?

– Ça dépend! Je n'aime pas quand un client met des heures à choisir un plat ou une bouteille de vin. Et je déteste les clients qui ne disent jamais 'merci' ou 's'il vous plaît'!

– À quelle heure finissez-vous votre travail?

– Vers onze heures du soir. Mais j'ai de la chance, car nous avons un excellent cuisinier et je prends tous mes repas du soir au restaurant.

– Vous êtes marié?

– Oui.

– Et qu'en pense votre femme?

– Elle est très contente. Elle déteste faire la cuisine!

Dix-septième unité

M. Brède	C'est un petit restaurant bien sympathique!
Mme Brède	Je voudrais une table près de la fenêtre.
M. Brède	Impossible! Elles sont toutes occupées. Regarde, il y a une petite table pour deux, dans le coin.
Mme Brède	La nappe est sale!
M. Brède	Je vais demander à la serveuse de la changer, quand je vais commander l'apéritif – Madame, s'il vous plaît!

Quelques minutes plus tard

Serveuse	Voilà messieurs-dames. Un kir et un whisky.
M. Brède	Merci.
Mme Brède	Charles, regarde, mon verre est fêlé, c'est dangereux!
M. Brède	Attends, j'appelle la serveuse.

Quelques minutes plus tard

Mme Brède	J'ai faim! Le service n'est pas très rapide.
M. Brède	Un peu de patience! Ah, voilà ton coq au vin!
Serveuse	Le coq au vin?
Mme Brède	C'est pour moi. Hmm, ça sent bon!
Serveuse	Et le bœuf bourguignon, pour monsieur. Bon appétit messieurs-dames!
M. Brède	Merci.
Mme Brède	Oh, quelle horreur!
M. Brède	Qu'est-ce qu'il y a?
Mme Brède	C'est froid!
M. Brède	Et moi, je n'ai pas de fourchette! Attends. Madame, s'il vous plaît!

Quelques minutes plus tard

Mme Brède   Oh, zut!

M. Brède   Quoi encore?

Mme Brède   Je viens de faire sauter de la sauce sur ma robe!

M. Brède   Mais, où est donc ta serviette?

Mme Brède   Je n'ai pas de serviette! Ah là là, quel restaurant!

M. Brède   Madame, s'il vous plaît!

À la fin du repas

Serveuse   Voilà l'addition messieurs-dames.

M. Brède   Merci…Mais, mais…ce n'est pas possible!

Mme Brède   Fais voir…Caviar…Champagne…Madame, s'il vous plaît!

Serveuse   Je suis désolée, messieurs-dames, c'est l'addition du couple qui célèbre un anniversaire de mariage!

Dix-huitième unité

1 – Vous vous habillez avant ou après le petit déjeuner?

   – Je m'habille après le petit déjeuner.

2 – Bonjour. Comment vous appelez-vous?

   – Je m'appelle Delphine. Et vous?

   – Moi, je m'appelle Alain.

3 – Vous vous levez à quelle heure?

   – En semaine, quand je vais travailler, je me lève à 7 heures. Le samedi et le dimanche je reste au lit jusqu'à midi!

4 – Vous vous brossez les dents combien de fois par jour?

   – Deux fois par jour, le matin et le soir.

5 – Qu'est-ce que vous regardez à la télévision?
   – J'aime les informations, les documentaires et les films.
   – Et votre mari?
   – Je ne sais pas. Il s'endort toujours devant la télévision!
6 – Combien de fois par semaine vous lavez-vous les cheveux?
   – Ça dépend, deux ou trois fois.
7 – Est-ce que vous vous maquillez tous les jours?
   – Je me maquille pour aller travailler et pour sortir. En général, je ne me maquille pas le dimanche.
8 – Vous vous réveillez à quelle heure le matin?
   – À 6 heures; le réveil sonne à 6 heures.
9 – Vos enfants se couchent à quelle heure?
   – Ils sont petits, ils vont au lit à 8 heures.
10 – Pardon, monsieur. Est-ce que vous vous rasez le matin ou le soir?
   – Je me rase tous les matins, sauf pendant les vacances.

Dix-neuvième unité

1 – Alors les enfants, où êtes-vous allés hier?
   – On est allé à la bibliothèque.
   – Ah, très bien! Et qu'est-ce que vous avez lu?
   – On a lu des bandes dessinées.
2 – Salut Bernard! Ça va? Qu'est-ce que tu as fait samedi dernier?
   – J'ai mangé un repas chinois, hmm, délicieux!
   – Ah bon, où ça?
   – Chez des amis.

3 – Bonjour Annette! Où êtes-vous allée le week-end dernier?
  – Je suis allée à Londres.
  – Formidable! Alors, qu'est-ce que vous avez fait à Londres?
  – Eh bien, j'ai visité la Tour de Londres et puis j'ai acheté des vêtements.
4 – Bonjour Monsieur Roquand. Comment allez-vous?
  – Très bien, merci, je suis en pleine forme. J'étais en vacances la semaine dernière!
  – Vous avez de la chance! Où êtes-vous allé?
  – Dans les Alpes. J'ai fait du ski pour la première fois de ma vie!
5 – Madame Orgerit, avez-vous regardé la télévision mardi soir?
  – Voyons…Mardi…Eh oui, je suis restée à la maison et j'ai regardé les informations et un film américain.

Vingtième unité

les parties du corps (p.288) Montrez la tête d'Odile. Montrez son bras droit. Montrez ses épaules. Montrez sa jambe gauche. Montrez ses mains. Montrez ses yeux. Montrez son œil gauche. Montrez son nez. Montrez sa bouche. Montrez son ventre. Montrez ses hanches. Montrez son oreille droite. Et finalement, montrez les genoux d'Odile.

Première partie 1 Asseyez-vous! **2** Fermez les yeux! **3** Respirez à fond! **4** Tournez la tête à droite, puis à gauche! **5** Levez-vous! **6** Pliez les genoux! **7** Touchez vos pieds! **8** Levez la jambe droite, puis la gauche. **9** Couchez-vous sur le dos et… **10** Reposez-vous un moment!

Deuxième partie

1 Les enfants ont mal au cœur en voiture.
   – Donnez-leur ces pillules une demi-heure avant le départ.
2 J'ai mal à la tête.
   – Prenez de l'aspirine.
3 Je voudrais quelque chose contre les piqûres de moustiques.
   – Mettez cette crème protectrice.
4 Ma fille tousse et elle a mal à la gorge.
   – Voilà des suppositoires.
5 J'ai de la fièvre.
   – Restez au lit et buvez beaucoup d'eau.
6 J'ai attrapé un coup de soleil.
   – Mettez cette lotion calmante.
7 J'ai mal au dos.
   – Reposez-vous, et prenez ces comprimés matin, midi et soir.
8 Je voudrais arrêter de fumer.
   – Essayez ces cigarettes aux herbes.

Vingt et unième unité

Première partie Je vais arriver à la gare à dix-huit heures. Je suis grande et mince. J'ai 32 ans. Je suis brune. J'ai les cheveux longs et raides. J'ai les yeux bleus et je porte des lunettes. Pour voyager je vais porter un pantalon noir et une veste rouge. J'ai un sac Vuitton et une énorme valise. J'espère que vous allez être au rendez-vous!

Deuxième partie

1 – Les enfants, vous voulez un paquet de bonbons ou une boîte de chocolats?
   – Une boîte de chocolats!

2 – Ma femme veut une bouteille de parfum pour son anniversaire.
   – Ça coûte cher, ça!
   – Je sais. Je lui ai acheté de l'eau de toilette.

3 – Vous avez une télévision en noir et blanc, madame Boussac?
   – Oui, elle est très vieille et elle tombe toujours en panne. Je veux m'acheter une télévision couleurs.

4 – Claudine, qu'est-ce que tu veux pour ton anniversaire?
   – Je veux un vélo, un vélo rouge.

5 – Mes parents veulent déménager. Leur maison est beaucoup trop grande maintenant.
   – Où veulent-ils aller?
   – Ils cherchent un appartement dans le Midi.

6 – Mon fils a dix-huit ans maintenant. Il vient d'avoir son permis de conduire et il veut une voiture.
   – Il veut une Petita, une Clio?
   – Pas du tout, il veut une voiture de sport!

7 – Philippe, qu'est-ce que tu veux faire à Noël?
   – Je veux aller aux sports d'hiver pour faire du ski. J'adore la neige.

8 – Qu'est-ce que vous allez donner à votre mari pour Noël?
   – Il adore la musique. Il veut des CD.

Troisième partie

– Est-ce que tu peux acheter le journal ce matin?
– Non, je ne peux pas sortir aujourd'hui, je suis malade.

– Vous allez aller en vacances à EuroDisney cette année?
– Je ne peux pas, ça coûte trop cher.

– Chéri, tu peux acheter une bouteille de champagne à midi pour fêter notre anniversaire de mariage?
– Je ne peux pas, la supérette ferme à l'heure du déjeuner.

– Les enfants, vous pouvez laver la voiture aujourd'hui?
– On ne peut pas, on doit faire nos devoirs.

– Sylvie, est-ce que vous pouvez téléphoner à la secrétaire de madame Berger?
– Non, je ne peux pas, je n'ai pas le temps.

– J'ai besoin d'argent pour faire les courses. Tu peux aller chercher trois cents euros à la banque?
– Je ne peux pas. C'est la fin du mois et nous n'avons plus d'argent!